APPLICATION DESIGN

KEY PRINCIPLES FOR DATA-INTENSIVE APP SYSTEMS

4 BOOKS IN 1

BOOK 1
FOUNDATIONS OF APPLICATION DESIGN: INTRODUCTION TO KEY PRINCIPLES FOR DATA-INTENSIVE SYSTEMS

BOOK 2
MASTERING DATA-INTENSIVE APP ARCHITECTURE: ADVANCED TECHNIQUES AND BEST PRACTICES

BOOK 3
SCALING APPLICATIONS: STRATEGIES AND TACTICS FOR HANDLING DATA-INTENSIVE WORKLOADS

BOOK 4
EXPERT INSIGHTS IN APPLICATION DESIGN: CUTTING-EDGE APPROACHES FOR DATA-INTENSIVE SYSTEMS

ROB BOTWRIGHT

Published by Rob Botwright
Library of Congress Cataloging-in-Publication Data
ISBN 978-1-83938-704-3
Cover design by Rizzo

Disclaimer

The contents of this book are based on extensive research and the best available historical sources. However, the author and publisher make no claims, promises, or guarantees about the accuracy, completeness, or adequacy of the information contained herein. The information in this book is provided on an "as is" basis, and the author and publisher disclaim any and all liability for any errors, omissions, or inaccuracies in the information or for any actions taken in reliance on such information. The opinions and views expressed in this book are those of the author and do not necessarily reflect the official policy or position of any organization or individual mentioned in this book. Any reference to specific people, places, or events is intended only to provide historical context and is not intended to defame or malign any group, individual, or entity. The information in this book is intended for educational and entertainment purposes only. It is not intended to be a substitute for professional advice or judgment. Readers are encouraged to conduct their own research and to seek professional advice where appropriate. Every effort has been made to obtain necessary permissions and acknowledgments for all images and other copyrighted material used in this book. Any errors or omissions in this regard are unintentional, and the author and publisher will correct them in future editions.

BOOK 1 - FOUNDATIONS OF APPLICATION DESIGN: INTRODUCTION TO KEY PRINCIPLES FOR DATA-INTENSIVE SYSTEMS

Introduction 5
Chapter 1: Understanding Data-Intensive Systems 8
Chapter 2: Principles of Application Architecture 14
Chapter 3: Data Modeling Fundamentals 20
Chapter 4: Introduction to Scalability Concepts 26
Chapter 5: Reliability and Fault Tolerance Basics 33
Chapter 6: Essential Tools for Data-Intensive Applications 43
Chapter 7: Security Considerations in Application Design 47
Chapter 8: Performance Optimization Techniques 57
Chapter 9: Integration Strategies for Data-Intensive Systems 65
Chapter 10: Future Trends in Application Design 74

BOOK 1 - FOUNDATIONS OF APPLICATION DESIGN: INTRODUCTION TO KEY PRINCIPLES FOR DATA-INTENSIVE SYSTEMS

Chapter 1: Advanced Data Modeling Strategies 83
Chapter 2: Scalability Patterns and Approaches 92
Chapter 3: Fault Tolerance in Complex Architectures 101
Chapter 4: Stream Processing and Real-Time Analytics 109
Chapter 5: Distributed Systems Design 117
Chapter 6: Containerization and Orchestration for App Deployment 124
Chapter 7: Microservices Architecture: Design and Implementation 132
Chapter 8: Performance Tuning in High-Volume Environments 140
Chapter 9: Advanced Security Protocols and Practices 148
Chapter 10: Governance and Compliance in Data-Intensive Appli 156

BOOK 1 - FOUNDATIONS OF APPLICATION DESIGN: INTRODUCTION TO KEY PRINCIPLES FOR DATA-INTENSIVE SYSTEMS

Chapter 1: Understanding Scalability in Application Design 165
Chapter 2: Horizontal and Vertical Scaling Techniques 173
Chapter 3: Load Balancing Strategies for Distributed Systems 180
Chapter 4: Caching and Data Replication for Improved Performance 187
Chapter 5: Elasticity and Auto-scaling in Cloud Environments 194
Chapter 6: Database Sharding and Partitioning 201
Chapter 7: Asynchronous Processing for Handling Bursty Workloads 207
Chapter 8: Scalable Data Storage Solutions 214
Chapter 9: High Availability Architectures for Resilience 219
Chapter 10: Monitoring and Performance Optimization at Scale 225

BOOK 1 - FOUNDATIONS OF APPLICATION DESIGN: INTRODUCTION TO KEY PRINCIPLES FOR DATA-INTENSIVE SYSTEMS

Chapter 1: Next-Generation Architectural Paradigms 232
Chapter 2: Advanced Data Processing Techniques 239
Chapter 3: Machine Learning Integration in Application Design 247
Chapter 4: Event-Driven Architectures for Real-Time Analytics 254
Chapter 5: Quantum Computing Applications in Data-Intensive Systems 261
Chapter 6: Blockchain Integration for Data Security and Integrity 267
Chapter 7: Serverless Computing and Function as a Service (FaaS) 273
Chapter 8: Edge Computing Strategies for Low-Latency Processing 279
Chapter 9: AI-Driven Automation in Application Deployment and Management 286
Chapter 10: Ethics and Governance in Emerging Technologies 293
Conclusion 300

Introduction

Welcome to the "Application Design: Key Principles for Data-Intensive App Systems" book bundle, a comprehensive collection of resources aimed at guiding you through the intricate world of designing and scaling data-intensive applications. In today's digital landscape, where data plays a central role in driving innovation and creating value, mastering the principles and techniques of application design is essential for building robust, scalable, and efficient systems.

This book bundle comprises four volumes, each addressing different aspects of application design for data-intensive systems:

Book 1 - Foundations of Application Design: Introduction to Key Principles for Data-Intensive Systems Book 2 - Mastering Data-Intensive App Architecture: Advanced Techniques and Best Practices Book 3 - Scaling Applications: Strategies and Tactics for Handling Data-Intensive Workloads Book 4 - Expert Insights in Application Design: Cutting-Edge Approaches for Data-Intensive Systems

In "Foundations of Application Design," you will embark on a journey to explore the fundamental principles that underpin the design of data-intensive systems. From understanding the basics of data modeling to exploring architecture patterns and scalability considerations, this introductory volume lays the groundwork for mastering the intricacies of application design.

Moving on to "Mastering Data-Intensive App Architecture," you will delve deeper into advanced techniques and best practices for architecting data-intensive applications. Topics such as distributed systems, microservices architecture, and optimization strategies will be covered in detail, providing you with the knowledge and skills needed to design scalable and resilient systems that can handle large-scale data workloads.

In "Scaling Applications," the focus shifts to strategies and tactics for effectively scaling applications to meet the demands of growing data volumes and user traffic. From performance optimization techniques to leveraging cloud computing and containerization technologies, this volume equips you with the tools and strategies needed to scale your applications efficiently and reliably.

Finally, in "Expert Insights in Application Design," you will gain valuable insights from industry experts and thought leaders in the field of application design. Through interviews, case studies, and analysis of emerging trends, you will learn about cutting-edge approaches and innovations shaping the future of data-intensive application development.

Whether you are a seasoned software engineer, an architect, or a technology leader, this book bundle offers valuable insights and practical guidance to help you navigate the complexities of designing and scaling data-intensive applications effectively. We hope that you find this collection of resources valuable in your journey to becoming a proficient application designer in the era of data-intensive computing.

BOOK 1
FOUNDATIONS OF APPLICATION DESIGN: INTRODUCTION
TO KEY PRINCIPLES FOR DATA-INTENSIVE SYSTEMS

ROB BOTWRIGHT

Chapter 1: Understanding Data-Intensive Systems

Data Processing Pipelines are integral components in modern data architecture, orchestrating the flow of data from various sources through a series of processing steps to derive valuable insights or facilitate downstream applications. These pipelines serve as the backbone of data-driven organizations, enabling them to handle vast amounts of data efficiently and effectively. A typical data processing pipeline comprises several stages, each tailored to perform specific tasks, including data ingestion, transformation, analysis, and storage. One popular framework for building data processing pipelines is Apache Kafka, which provides a distributed messaging system capable of handling high-throughput data streams. To deploy a data processing pipeline using Kafka, start by setting up a Kafka cluster using the following CLI command:

bashCopy code

```
bin/zookeeper-server-start.sh
config/zookeeper.properties
```

This command launches the Zookeeper service, a critical component for coordinating distributed systems like Kafka. Next, start the Kafka broker using:

bashCopy code

```
bin/kafka-server-start.sh config/server.properties
```

With Kafka up and running, data ingestion can commence. Producers publish data to Kafka topics, while consumers subscribe to these topics to process the incoming data. Kafka's distributed nature allows for horizontal scaling,

ensuring scalability and fault tolerance. Once data is ingested into Kafka, it can be processed using various tools and frameworks like Apache Spark or Apache Flink. These frameworks offer robust libraries for data manipulation, enabling tasks such as filtering, aggregating, and joining datasets. For instance, to deploy a Spark job to process data from Kafka, use the following command:
bashCopy code

```
spark-submit --class com.example.DataProcessor --master spark://<spark-master>:7077 --jars spark-streaming-kafka-0-8-assembly.jar my-data-processing-app.jar
```

This command submits a Spark job to the Spark cluster, specifying the entry class, master node, and necessary dependencies. Spark then processes the data in parallel across the cluster, leveraging its distributed computing capabilities for high performance. As data is processed, it may undergo transformations to cleanse, enrich, or aggregate it, preparing it for downstream analysis or storage. After processing, the data can be persisted to various storage systems, including relational databases, data lakes, or cloud storage services. For example, to store processed data in a MySQL database, use the following SQL command:
sqlCopy code

```
INSERT INTO table_name (column1, column2, ...) VALUES (value1, value2, ...);
```

This command inserts the processed data into the specified table in the MySQL database, making it accessible for further analysis or reporting. Additionally, data processing pipelines often incorporate monitoring and logging mechanisms to track the pipeline's health and performance. Tools like Prometheus and Grafana can be used to monitor Kafka cluster metrics, while ELK stack (Elasticsearch, Logstash, and Kibana) can centralize logs for easy analysis and troubleshooting. By implementing robust data processing pipelines, organizations can unlock the value hidden within their data, driving informed decision-making and innovation.

Big data technologies have revolutionized the way organizations collect, store, process, and analyze vast amounts of data to derive valuable insights and drive informed decision-making. These technologies encompass a wide range of tools, frameworks, and platforms designed to tackle the challenges posed by the ever-growing volume, velocity, and variety of data generated in today's digital age. One of the fundamental components of big data technology is distributed computing, which enables the parallel processing of large datasets across multiple nodes or clusters of computers. Apache Hadoop is one of the pioneering frameworks in this space, providing a distributed storage and processing system for handling big data workloads. To deploy a Hadoop cluster, administrators can use the following CLI command:
bashCopy code

hadoop-deploy-cluster.sh

This command initiates the deployment process, configuring the Hadoop cluster with the specified settings and parameters. Once the cluster is up and running, users can leverage Hadoop's distributed file system (HDFS) to store large datasets and execute MapReduce jobs to process them in parallel. MapReduce is a programming model for processing and generating large datasets that consists of two phases: the map phase, where data is transformed into key-value pairs, and the reduce phase, where the output of the map phase is aggregated and summarized. To run a MapReduce job on a Hadoop cluster, use the following command:

bashCopy code

```
hadoop    jar    path/to/hadoop-mapreduce-job.jar
input_path output_path
```

This command submits the MapReduce job to the Hadoop cluster, specifying the input and output paths for the data. As the job executes, Hadoop distributes the processing tasks across the cluster nodes, enabling efficient data processing at scale. In addition to Hadoop, other distributed computing frameworks have emerged to address specific use cases and requirements in the big data landscape. Apache Spark, for example, offers in-memory processing capabilities that significantly improve performance compared to traditional disk-based processing models. To deploy a Spark cluster, use the following command:

bashCopy code

```
spark-deploy-cluster.sh
```

This command initializes a Spark cluster, allowing users to execute complex data processing tasks, including batch processing, stream processing, machine learning, and graph analytics. Spark's rich set of APIs and libraries, such as Spark SQL, Spark Streaming, MLlib, and GraphX, make it a versatile framework for a wide range of big data applications. Another key aspect of big data technologies is data storage, which plays a crucial role in efficiently managing and accessing large datasets. NoSQL databases have gained popularity for their ability to handle unstructured and semi-structured data types at scale.

MongoDB, for instance, is a document-oriented NoSQL database that stores data in flexible, JSON-like documents. To deploy a MongoDB cluster, use the following command:

bashCopy code

mongo-deploy-cluster.sh

This command provisions a MongoDB cluster, allowing users to store and query data using MongoDB's powerful query language and indexing capabilities. MongoDB's distributed architecture ensures high availability and horizontal scalability, making it suitable for a variety of big data use cases, including content management, real-time analytics, and Internet of Things (IoT) applications. Additionally, cloud-based big data platforms have emerged as popular alternatives to on-premises infrastructure, offering scalability, flexibility, and cost-effectiveness for storing and processing large datasets. Amazon Web Services (AWS), Microsoft Azure, and Google Cloud Platform (GCP) are among the leading providers of cloud-based big data services. To deploy a big data cluster on AWS using Amazon EMR (Elastic MapReduce), use the following command:

bashCopy code

aws emr create-cluster --name my-cluster --release-label emr-6.3.0 --instance-type m5.xlarge --instance-count 5 -- applications Name=Spark Name=Hadoop Name=Hive

This command creates an EMR cluster on AWS, specifying the cluster name, EC2 instance type, instance count, and applications to install (e.g., Spark, Hadoop, Hive). Once the cluster is provisioned, users can leverage AWS EMR's managed services to run big data workloads, such as data processing, analytics, and machine learning, without the need to manage underlying infrastructure. In summary, big data technologies offer powerful tools and platforms for organizations to harness the potential of their data assets and gain actionable insights that drive business growth and innovation. From distributed computing frameworks like Hadoop and Spark to NoSQL databases like MongoDB and cloud-based services like Amazon EMR, the big data ecosystem continues to evolve, providing increasingly sophisticated solutions for addressing the challenges of the data-driven world.

Chapter 2: Principles of Application Architecture

Layered architecture is a fundamental design pattern commonly used in software development to structure complex systems in a hierarchical manner, facilitating modularity, scalability, and maintainability. At its core, layered architecture organizes software components into distinct layers, each responsible for specific functionalities, with higher layers depending on lower layers for services and functionality. This architectural style promotes separation of concerns, allowing developers to focus on implementing and managing individual layers independently, thus enhancing code reusability and promoting a clear separation of responsibilities. The layered architecture pattern typically consists of three main layers: presentation, business logic, and data access. To deploy a layered architecture, developers often start by defining the layers and their respective responsibilities. In the presentation layer, user interfaces and interaction components are implemented, providing users with a means to interact with the system. This layer handles user input and presents data to the user in a comprehensible format. One commonly used technology in the presentation layer is HTML/CSS/JavaScript for web applications. Developers use HTML to structure the content, CSS to style it, and JavaScript to add interactivity. For example, to create a basic HTML file, one can use the following command:
bashCopy code

```
touch index.html
```

This command creates a new HTML file named "index.html" in the current directory. Moving on to the business logic layer, this layer contains the core functionality of the application, including algorithms, calculations, and business rules. It orchestrates the flow of data between the presentation layer and the data access layer, processing requests, and generating responses. Object-oriented programming languages like Java or C# are commonly used to implement the business logic layer. In Java, for instance, one can create a class to represent business logic:

bashCopy code

```
vim BusinessLogic.java
```

This command opens the Vim text editor to create a new Java file named "BusinessLogic.java". In this file, developers can define methods and functions to implement the business logic of the application. Finally, in the data access layer, data storage and retrieval mechanisms are implemented. This layer interacts with the underlying data storage systems, such as databases or file systems, to perform CRUD (Create, Read, Update, Delete) operations on data. SQL (Structured Query Language) is often used to interact with relational databases like MySQL or PostgreSQL. To install MySQL and create a new database, one can use the following commands:

bashCopy code

```
sudo apt-get update sudo apt-get install mysql-server
sudo mysql_secure_installation sudo mysql
```

These commands update the package repository, install MySQL server, secure the installation, and start the MySQL command-line client, respectively. Within the

MySQL command-line client, one can then create a new database:

sqlCopy code

```
CREATE DATABASE my_database;
```

This SQL command creates a new database named "my_database". Once the database is created, developers can define tables and perform data manipulation operations as needed. Additionally, NoSQL databases like MongoDB or Redis are popular choices for applications requiring flexible and scalable data storage. To install MongoDB, one can use the following commands:

bashCopy code

```
sudo apt-get install mongodb sudo systemctl start mongodb
```

These commands install MongoDB and start the MongoDB service, allowing developers to interact with the database using the MongoDB shell or a programming language-specific driver. In summary, layered architecture provides a structured approach to software design, promoting separation of concerns and facilitating modular development. By organizing components into distinct layers, developers can create scalable, maintainable, and extensible systems that are easier to understand, test, and maintain. Whether building web applications, enterprise systems, or mobile apps, the layered architecture pattern remains a valuable tool in the software engineer's toolkit, enabling the development of robust and resilient software solutions.

Microservices vs Monolithic Architecture is a pivotal consideration in modern software design, shaping the way applications are developed, deployed, and maintained.

Microservices architecture advocates for breaking down large, monolithic applications into smaller, loosely coupled services, each responsible for a specific business function or capability. In contrast, monolithic architecture consolidates all application functionality into a single, cohesive unit. Each approach has its advantages and drawbacks, making the choice between them a critical decision for software architects and developers. To better understand the differences between microservices and monolithic architecture, it's essential to delve into their respective characteristics, benefits, and challenges. In a monolithic architecture, the entire application is built as a single, interconnected unit, typically comprising multiple layers, such as presentation, business logic, and data access, tightly coupled together. This tight coupling can simplify development and testing initially, as developers can work within a unified codebase and easily share resources. However, as the application grows in complexity, monolithic architectures often encounter challenges related to scalability, maintainability, and agility. To deploy a monolithic application, developers typically compile the entire codebase into a single executable or deployable artifact, such as a WAR (Web Application Archive) file for Java applications. For example, to build and package a Java web application using Apache Maven, one can use the following command:

bashCopy code

```
mvn package
```

This command compiles the source code, runs tests, and packages the application into a WAR file, ready for deployment to a servlet container like Apache Tomcat or

Jetty. While monolithic architecture offers simplicity and familiarity, it can become a bottleneck as the application scales or evolves. Microservices architecture, on the other hand, advocates for decomposing the application into a collection of small, independent services, each encapsulating a specific business capability. These services communicate with each other through well-defined APIs (Application Programming Interfaces), enabling them to evolve and scale independently. By decoupling services, microservices architecture promotes flexibility, resilience, and agility, allowing teams to develop, deploy, and maintain services autonomously. To deploy a microservices-based application, developers typically containerize each service using technologies like Docker and manage them using orchestration platforms like Kubernetes. For instance, to containerize a Node.js microservice using Docker, one can create a Dockerfile:
DockerfileCopy code

```
FROM    node:14    WORKDIR    /usr/src/app    COPY
package*.json ./ RUN npm install COPY . . EXPOSE 3000
CMD ["node", "index.js"]
```

This Dockerfile defines a Docker image for a Node.js microservice, copying the source code into the container and exposing port 3000 for communication. To build the Docker image, use the following command:
bashCopy code

```
docker build -t my-node-service .
```

This command builds a Docker image named "my-node-service" based on the instructions in the Dockerfile. Once the image is built, it can be deployed to a container orchestration platform like Kubernetes for management and scaling. While microservices architecture offers benefits in terms of scalability, resilience, and agility, it also introduces complexities in terms of distributed systems, service communication, and data management. Additionally, managing a large number of services can incur overhead in terms of monitoring, deployment, and coordination. Furthermore, transitioning from a monolithic architecture to a microservices-based approach requires careful planning, refactoring, and cultural shifts within organizations. In summary, the choice between microservices and monolithic architecture depends on various factors, including the nature of the application, organizational goals, and development team's expertise. Both approaches have their place in software development, and the decision should be made based on a thorough understanding of their strengths, weaknesses, and trade-offs. Ultimately, successful software architecture involves selecting the right architectural style that aligns with the application's requirements and the organization's strategic objectives.

Chapter 3: Data Modeling Fundamentals

Entity-Relationship (ER) Modeling is a crucial aspect of database design, providing a visual representation of the data structure and relationships within a database system. It serves as a blueprint for designing databases, enabling developers to conceptualize and organize the data model effectively. In ER modeling, entities represent real-world objects or concepts, while relationships define the associations between these entities. Attributes further describe the properties or characteristics of entities, providing additional context and detail. The primary goal of ER modeling is to create a clear and concise representation of the data requirements, facilitating the development of well-structured and efficient databases. To begin an ER modeling process, developers often use diagramming tools like Lucidchart, Microsoft Visio, or draw.io to create visual representations of the database schema. These tools offer intuitive interfaces for designing ER diagrams, allowing users to drag and drop entities, relationships, and attributes onto the canvas. For example, to create an ER diagram using draw.io, users can navigate to the website and select the "Entity Relationship" template to get started. Once the template is opened, users can add entities by dragging the "Entity" shape onto the canvas and double-clicking to edit the entity name. Attributes can be added by clicking on the entity and selecting "Add Attribute" from the context menu, allowing users to define the properties of each entity. Relationships between entities can be established by selecting the "Line" tool and drawing connections between related entities, specifying cardinality and relationship types as needed. Once the ER diagram is complete, developers can export it as an image or PDF file for documentation purposes or share it with stakeholders for review. In addition to visual tools, developers can also use textual representations like Entity-Relationship Diagram (ERD) notation to describe database schemas using plain text. This notation employs symbols such as rectangles for entities, diamonds for relationships, and ovals for attributes, making it easy to represent complex data structures in a concise format. For instance, an ERD notation for a simple library database might look like this: scssCopy code

Book (ISBN, Title, Author) Member (ID, Name, Address) Borrow (ID, ISBN, Member_ID, Borrow_Date, Return_Date)

In this example, "Book," "Member," and "Borrow" represent entities, while attributes like "ISBN," "Title," and "Author" describe the properties of the Book entity. Relationships between entities, such as the Borrow relationship between Book and Member, are represented by connecting lines, with cardinality constraints specifying the nature of the relationship. ER modeling also encompasses various concepts and techniques to enhance the clarity and effectiveness of the data model. For example, normalization is a process used to organize data into tables and eliminate redundancy, ensuring data integrity and minimizing storage space. Developers can use normalization techniques like First Normal Form (1NF), Second Normal Form (2NF), and Third Normal Form (3NF) to structure databases efficiently. To normalize a database, developers can follow a step-by-step process to identify repeating groups, dependencies, and candidate keys, then apply normalization rules to eliminate anomalies and ensure data integrity. Another important aspect of ER modeling is the identification of entity relationships, including one-to-one, one-to-many, and many-to-many relationships. Cardinality constraints specify the number of instances of one entity that can be associated with another entity, helping to define the nature of the relationship accurately. For instance, a one-to-many relationship between a Department entity and an Employee entity implies that each department can have multiple employees, while each employee belongs to only one department. Developers can use symbols like "1" and "N" to denote cardinality constraints in ER diagrams, clarifying the relationships between entities. Overall, Entity-Relationship Modeling is a fundamental technique in database design, providing a structured approach to defining data models and relationships. By creating clear and concise representations of the data structure, developers can design databases that meet the requirements of the application, promote data integrity, and support efficient data retrieval and manipulation. Whether using visual diagramming tools or textual notations, ER modeling enables developers to communicate and collaborate effectively on database design, laying the foundation for robust and scalable database systems. Normalization and denormalization are essential techniques in database design, aimed at organizing and optimizing data structures for efficient storage, retrieval, and manipulation. Normalization involves breaking down a database schema into smaller, well-structured tables to eliminate redundancy and dependency anomalies, ensuring data integrity and minimizing data redundancy. Denormalization, on the other hand, involves combining tables and duplicating data to optimize query performance and simplify data retrieval. These techniques play a critical role in designing databases that meet the requirements of the application and support scalability, flexibility, and performance. To begin with normalization, developers often follow a set of normalization rules, such as the ones defined by Edgar F. Codd, to systematically organize data and eliminate data anomalies. The normalization process typically involves multiple stages, each aimed at achieving a specific level of normalization, known as normal forms. One of the most commonly used normal forms is the First Normal Form (1NF), which requires eliminating repeating groups and ensuring atomicity of attributes. To transform a table into 1NF, developers identify repeating groups or multivalued attributes and create separate tables for them. For example, consider a table storing customer information with repeating phone numbers:

```
diffCopy code
Customer_ID | Name | Phone_Numbers ------------|---------
-|--------------- 1 | John Doe | 123-456-7890, 987-654-3210
```

To normalize this table into 1NF, developers create a separate table to store phone numbers:

```
diffCopy code
Customer_ID | Phone_Number ------------|--------------- 1 |
123-456-7890 1 | 987-654-3210
```

This transformation ensures atomicity of attributes and eliminates repeating groups, bringing the table into 1NF. Moving on to higher normal forms, developers aim to eliminate transitive dependencies and partial dependencies, ensuring data integrity and reducing redundancy further. The Second Normal Form (2NF) requires that every non-key attribute is fully functionally dependent on the entire primary key. To achieve 2NF, developers identify and remove partial dependencies by creating separate tables for related attributes. For example, consider a table storing employee information with attributes Employee_ID, Department_ID, and Department_Name:

```
diffCopy code
Employee_ID | Department_ID | Department_Name ------
------|---------------|---------------- 1 | 101 | Marketing 2 |
102 | Sales 3 | 101 | Marketing
```

In this table, Department_Name is functionally dependent on Department_ID but not on Employee_ID, resulting in a partial dependency. To normalize this table into 2NF, developers create a separate table for departments:

```
diffCopy code
Department_ID | Department_Name -------------|-----------
----- 101 | Marketing 102 | Sales
```

This separation ensures that Department_Name is fully functionally dependent on Department_ID, meeting the requirements of 2NF. Continuing the normalization process, developers aim to achieve higher normal forms, such as Third Normal Form (3NF) and Boyce-Codd Normal Form (BCNF), to further eliminate dependencies and redundancy. While normalization helps ensure data integrity and minimize redundancy, it can sometimes lead to performance issues, especially in read-heavy applications where complex joins are required to retrieve data. Denormalization addresses this issue by reintroducing redundancy and combining tables to optimize query performance and simplify data retrieval. Denormalization techniques include materialized views, redundant columns, and precomputed aggregates, which store redundant data to avoid costly join operations and improve query performance. For example, consider a denormalized schema storing customer orders with redundant customer information:

```yaml
yaml Copy code
Order_ID  |  Customer_ID  |  Customer_Name  |  Order_Date  |  Total_Amount
--------- | ------------- | ----------- | ---- | ------------ | -------------
1 | 101 | John Doe | 2023-01-01 | 100.00
2 | 102 | Jane Smith | 2023-01-02 | 150.00
3 | 101 | John Doe | 2023-01-03 | 200.00
```

In this denormalized schema, Customer_Name is duplicated in each row, eliminating the need for a separate table to store customer information. While denormalization can improve query performance, it also introduces risks such as data redundancy and inconsistency, as updates to redundant data must be propagated across all copies. Therefore, developers must carefully consider the trade-offs between normalization and denormalization based on the requirements of the application, the frequency of data updates, and the performance constraints. In summary, normalization and denormalization are essential techniques in database design, each serving distinct purposes in optimizing data structures for efficiency and performance.

Chapter 4: Introduction to Scalability Concepts

Horizontal scaling and vertical scaling are two distinct approaches to increasing the capacity and performance of a system, each offering unique advantages and challenges. Horizontal scaling, also known as scaling out, involves adding more instances of resources, such as servers or nodes, to distribute the workload across multiple machines. In contrast, vertical scaling, or scaling up, involves upgrading the existing resources, such as CPU, memory, or storage, to handle increased demands. Both scaling strategies have their place in system architecture and are utilized based on factors such as performance requirements, cost considerations, and scalability goals. To understand horizontal scaling, consider a scenario where a web application experiences increasing traffic and load on its servers. Instead of upgrading the existing server hardware, the system administrators opt for horizontal scaling by adding more servers to the server pool. This can be achieved by provisioning additional virtual machines or containers to handle incoming requests. One popular tool for managing horizontal scaling is Kubernetes, an open-source container orchestration platform that automates the deployment, scaling, and management of containerized applications. To deploy a horizontally scaled application using Kubernetes, developers can define a deployment configuration file specifying the desired number of replicas, or instances, of the application:
bashCopy code

```
kubectl create deployment my-app --image=my-app-
image --replicas=3
```

This command creates a Kubernetes deployment named "my-app" with three replicas of the "my-app-image" container image. Kubernetes automatically schedules these replicas across the available nodes in the cluster, distributing the workload evenly. Horizontal scaling offers several benefits, including improved fault tolerance, increased availability, and better performance under high traffic conditions. By distributing the workload across multiple instances, horizontal scaling reduces the risk of a single point of failure and ensures that the system can handle spikes in traffic without degradation in performance. However, horizontal scaling also introduces challenges, such as managing distributed systems, synchronizing data across instances, and ensuring consistency and coherence in the application state. To address these challenges, developers often employ techniques like load balancing, data partitioning, and distributed caching. Load balancing distributes incoming requests across multiple instances, ensuring that no single instance becomes overloaded. Tools like Nginx or HAProxy can be used to implement load balancing in a horizontally scaled environment:

bashCopy code

```
sudo apt-get install nginx
```

This command installs the Nginx web server, which can be configured as a reverse proxy to distribute incoming HTTP requests to multiple backend servers. Data partitioning involves dividing the dataset into smaller, manageable chunks and distributing them across multiple servers. This allows for parallel processing and improved scalability, but

requires careful consideration of data distribution strategies and consistency guarantees. Distributed caching, using tools like Redis or Memcached, can improve performance by caching frequently accessed data closer to the application instances, reducing the need to fetch data from the backend storage. Vertical scaling, on the other hand, involves upgrading the existing resources of a single server to handle increased demands. This can include adding more CPU cores, increasing memory capacity, or upgrading storage devices. One common example of vertical scaling is upgrading the RAM of a database server to improve query performance and handle larger datasets. To upgrade the RAM of a server running Linux, administrators can use the following command to check the current memory configuration:
bashCopy code

```
sudo lshw -class memory
```

This command displays detailed information about the system's memory configuration, including the total amount of RAM installed and available slots for additional memory modules. Based on this information, administrators can purchase and install compatible memory modules to upgrade the server's RAM capacity. Vertical scaling offers simplicity and ease of management, as it involves upgrading a single server rather than managing a distributed system. It is often suitable for applications with low to moderate traffic volumes or those that require access to a centralized dataset. However, vertical scaling also has limitations, including scalability constraints, potential single points of failure, and diminishing returns on investment as resources become more expensive to upgrade. Additionally, vertical scaling may not be feasible for applications with highly variable or unpredictable workloads, as it requires forecasting future resource requirements and preemptively upgrading hardware. In summary, horizontal scaling and vertical scaling are two complementary approaches to increasing the capacity and performance of a system. Horizontal scaling distributes the workload across multiple instances to improve fault tolerance and scalability, while vertical scaling involves upgrading the existing resources of a single server to handle increased demands. By understanding the strengths and limitations of each approach, developers and system administrators can design scalable and resilient systems that meet the requirements of their applications.

Load balancing strategies are crucial components in distributed systems architecture, designed to distribute incoming traffic across multiple servers or resources to ensure optimal performance, availability, and scalability. As the volume of users and requests increases, load balancers play a critical role in efficiently managing and distributing the workload, preventing individual servers from becoming overwhelmed and ensuring that resources are utilized effectively. Various load balancing algorithms and techniques exist, each tailored to address specific requirements and characteristics of the application and infrastructure. One common load balancing strategy is round-robin, where incoming requests are evenly distributed across a pool of servers in a cyclic fashion. This ensures that each server receives an equal share of the workload, promoting fairness and balance in resource utilization. To configure round-robin load balancing using

Nginx, a popular open-source web server and reverse proxy, developers can define a server block in the Nginx configuration file with multiple upstream servers:

bashCopy code

```
sudo nano /etc/nginx/nginx.conf
```

This command opens the Nginx configuration file in the Nano text editor, allowing developers to define the server block. Within the server block, developers can define upstream servers using the "upstream" directive:

nginxCopy code

```
upstream myapp { server server1.example.com; server server2.example.com; server server3.example.com; }
```

In this configuration, Nginx defines an upstream group named "myapp" with three servers: server1.example.com, server2.example.com, and server3.example.com. To enable round-robin load balancing for incoming requests, developers can configure a location block to proxy requests to the upstream servers:

nginxCopy code

```
server { listen 80; server_name example.com; location / { proxy_pass http://myapp; } }
```

This configuration directs incoming requests to the "myapp" upstream group, distributing them across the defined servers in a round-robin fashion. Another commonly used load balancing strategy is least connections, where incoming requests are directed to the server with the fewest active connections at the time of the request. This ensures that the workload is evenly distributed based on the current server load, minimizing response times and maximizing resource utilization. To implement least connections load balancing with Nginx, developers can use the "least_conn" directive within the upstream block:

nginxCopy code

```
upstream myapp { least_conn; server server1.example.com; server server2.example.com; server server3.example.com; }
```

In this configuration, Nginx dynamically selects the server with the fewest active connections to handle each incoming request, ensuring efficient load distribution. Additionally, load balancing strategies can incorporate health checks to monitor the status and availability of backend servers, ensuring that requests are only directed to healthy and operational servers. Nginx provides health check capabilities through the "health_check" directive, allowing developers to define custom health check parameters and thresholds:

nginxCopy code

```
upstream myapp { server server1.example.com; server server2.example.com; server server3.example.com; health_check interval=5s timeout=2s fall=3 rise=2; }
```

In this configuration, Nginx performs health checks on the upstream servers every 5 seconds, with a timeout of 2 seconds for each check. If a server fails three consecutive health checks (fall=3), it is considered unhealthy, and Nginx stops routing requests to it until it passes two consecutive health checks (rise=2). By incorporating health checks into load balancing strategies, administrators can ensure high availability and reliability of the system, automatically routing traffic away from unhealthy or malfunctioning servers. Load balancing strategies can also take into account various factors such as server weights, geographic proximity, and session persistence to further optimize performance and user experience. For example, weighted load balancing assigns different weights to servers based on their capacity and capabilities, allowing administrators to prioritize certain servers over others. To configure weighted load balancing with Nginx, developers can specify weights for each server in the upstream block:

nginxCopy code

upstream myapp { server server1.example.com weight=2; server server2.example.com weight=1; server server3.example.com weight=1; }

In this configuration, Nginx assigns a weight of 2 to server1.example.com and weights of 1 to server2.example.com and server3.example.com, ensuring that server1 receives twice as much traffic as the other servers. Load balancing strategies can be further customized and fine-tuned to meet the specific requirements and objectives of the application and infrastructure. By selecting the appropriate load balancing algorithm and parameters, administrators can optimize resource utilization, improve scalability, and enhance the overall performance and availability of the system.

Chapter 5: Reliability and Fault Tolerance Basics

Redundancy and replication are fundamental concepts in system design and data management, aimed at enhancing reliability, fault tolerance, and availability. Redundancy involves duplicating critical components or resources within a system to ensure that there are backups in case of failures or outages. Replication, on the other hand, involves creating and maintaining multiple copies of data or resources across different locations or nodes, ensuring that data is consistently available and accessible. These techniques are widely used in various domains, including computer networks, distributed systems, and database management, to mitigate the impact of failures and improve system resilience. In computer networks, redundancy is employed to ensure continuous connectivity and minimize the risk of network outages. For example, network administrators often deploy redundant network links, switches, and routers to create redundant paths and eliminate single points of failure. Spanning Tree Protocol (STP) is a common network protocol used to manage redundancy and prevent network loops in Ethernet networks. To enable STP on a Cisco switch, administrators can use the following CLI commands:
bashCopy code
enable configure terminal spanning-tree mode rapid-pvst
These commands enable rapid spanning tree mode (Rapid PVST+) on the switch, allowing it to detect and prevent network loops by selectively blocking redundant links. By deploying redundant network infrastructure and

protocols, organizations can ensure continuous connectivity and minimize downtime, even in the event of hardware failures or network disruptions. In distributed systems and cloud computing environments, redundancy and replication are essential for achieving high availability and fault tolerance. Distributed systems distribute computing tasks across multiple nodes to improve scalability and reliability. Redundant nodes are deployed to handle failover in case of node failures, ensuring that the system remains operational and responsive. For example, in a Kubernetes cluster, administrators can deploy redundant instances of application pods across multiple nodes to ensure continuous availability. To deploy a replicated application using Kubernetes, developers can define a replication controller or deployment configuration specifying the desired number of replicas:

bashCopy code

```
kubectl create deployment my-app --image=my-app-image --replicas=3
```

This command creates a Kubernetes deployment named "my-app" with three replicas of the "my-app-image" container image, distributing the workload across multiple instances for redundancy and fault tolerance. In database management systems, replication is used to ensure data durability and availability by maintaining multiple copies of data across different nodes or data centers. Replication techniques such as master-slave replication and multi-master replication are commonly used to synchronize data between database instances and ensure consistency. For instance, in MySQL, administrators can configure master-slave replication by setting up a master database server to replicate data changes to one or more slave servers. To configure master-slave replication in MySQL, administrators can use the following CLI commands on the master server:

bashCopy code

```
mysql -u root -p
```

This command opens the MySQL command-line client and prompts for the root password. Once logged in, administrators can execute SQL commands to configure replication:

sqlCopy code

```
CREATE USER 'replication_user'@'%' IDENTIFIED BY 'password'; GRANT REPLICATION SLAVE ON *.* TO 'replication_user'@'%'; FLUSH PRIVILEGES; SHOW MASTER STATUS;
```

These commands create a replication user, grant replication privileges, and display the current master status, including the binary log file name and position. On the slave server, administrators can use the following CLI commands to configure replication:

bashCopy code

```
CHANGE MASTER TO MASTER_HOST='master_host',
MASTER_USER='replication_user',
MASTER_PASSWORD='password',
MASTER_LOG_FILE='binlog_file',
MASTER_LOG_POS=binlog_position; START SLAVE;
```

These commands configure the slave server to replicate data changes from the master server and start the replication process. By deploying master-slave replication, organizations can ensure data redundancy and availability, with failover capabilities to withstand node failures or data center outages. In summary, redundancy and replication are essential techniques for enhancing reliability, fault tolerance, and availability in computer networks, distributed systems, and database management. By deploying redundant components and maintaining multiple copies of data, organizations can minimize the impact of failures and ensure continuous operation even in the face of hardware failures, network outages, or data corruption. Whether deploying redundant network links, redundant nodes in distributed systems, or replicated databases, redundancy and replication are critical components of resilient and highly available systems.

Error handling and failure recovery mechanisms are critical components of software and system design, essential for ensuring system reliability, availability, and fault tolerance. Error handling involves detecting, reporting, and responding to errors or exceptional conditions that occur during program execution, while failure recovery mechanisms focus on restoring system functionality and data integrity in the event of failures or errors. These mechanisms are essential for mitigating the impact of unexpected events, such as hardware failures, software bugs, network disruptions, or data corruption, and play a vital role in maintaining system stability and performance.

In software development, error handling begins with identifying potential sources of errors and defining strategies to handle them gracefully. Developers employ techniques such as exception handling, error codes, assertions, and logging to manage errors effectively.

Exception handling, a commonly used approach, involves catching and handling exceptions, or runtime errors, that occur during program execution. In languages like Java, developers use try-catch blocks to encapsulate code that may throw exceptions and handle them gracefully:

javaCopy code

```
try { // code that may throw exceptions } catch (Exception e) { // handle the exception }
```

This code structure allows developers to catch exceptions and take appropriate actions, such as logging the error, retrying the operation, or providing user feedback. Error codes are another approach to error handling, where functions return numeric or symbolic error codes to indicate the success or failure of an operation. Developers can use these error codes to determine the cause of errors and take corrective actions accordingly. Assertions are used to enforce conditions that must be true at specific points in the code, helping to identify and address errors early in the development process. Logging is essential for recording error messages, stack traces, and diagnostic information for debugging and troubleshooting purposes. Developers use logging frameworks like Log4j or Logback to log error messages to files, consoles, or remote servers:

javaCopy code

```
Logger logger = LoggerFactory.getLogger(MyClass.class);
logger.error("An error occurred: {}", exception.getMessage(), exception);
```

This code snippet logs an error message along with the exception stack trace using the SLF4J logging framework in Java.

In addition to error handling techniques, failure recovery mechanisms are essential for restoring system functionality and data integrity in the event of failures. These mechanisms include techniques such as retries, timeouts, redundancy, and checkpointing. Retries involve automatically retrying failed operations to increase the likelihood of success. For example, in distributed systems, clients may retry failed requests to remote services with exponential backoff and jitter to avoid overwhelming the server:

pythonCopy code

```
import time import random max_retries = 3 retry_delay
= 1 # seconds for attempt in range(max_retries): try: #
code that may fail break # if successful, exit the loop
except Exception as e: print(f"Error: {e}. Retrying in
{retry_delay} seconds...") time.sleep(retry_delay)
retry_delay *= 2 + random.uniform(-0.5, 0.5) #
exponential backoff with jitter
```

This Python code retries a failed operation with exponential backoff and jitter, increasing the delay between retries to reduce the likelihood of congestion and retries synchronization.

Timeouts are another important failure recovery mechanism used to limit the duration of operations and prevent them from hanging indefinitely. Developers specify timeout values for network requests, database queries, or other potentially blocking operations to ensure timely responses and prevent resource exhaustion. For example, in Python's requests library, developers can set a timeout parameter when making HTTP requests:

pythonCopy code

```python
import requests url = "https://example.com" timeout = 5
# seconds try: response = requests.get(url,
timeout=timeout) response.raise_for_status() # raise an
error for non-200 status codes print("Request
succeeded:", response.text) except requests.Timeout:
print("Request timed out after", timeout, "seconds")
except requests.RequestException as e: print("Request
failed:", e)
```

This Python code sets a timeout of 5 seconds for an HTTP
GET request to "https://example.com" using the requests
library, handling timeout and other request-related
exceptions gracefully.

Redundancy is a common strategy for failure recovery,
involving the duplication of critical components or
resources to ensure that backups are available in case of
failures. Redundancy can be applied at various levels,
including hardware redundancy, software redundancy,
and data redundancy. Hardware redundancy involves
deploying redundant hardware components, such as
servers, storage devices, or network links, to eliminate
single points of failure and ensure continuous operation.
For example, in a redundant array of independent disks
(RAID) configuration, data is distributed across multiple
disks, with redundancy mechanisms like mirroring or
parity to protect against disk failures:

bashCopy code

```bash
mdadm --create /dev/md0 --level=1 --raid-devices=2
/dev/sda1 /dev/sdb1
```

This command creates a RAID-1 array named /dev/md0
with two disks (/dev/sda1 and /dev/sdb1) using the

mdadm utility in Linux, configuring mirroring for redundancy.

Software redundancy involves replicating critical software components, such as application servers or microservices, across multiple nodes or instances to ensure continuous availability and fault tolerance. For example, in a Kubernetes cluster, administrators can deploy multiple replicas of an application using a deployment configuration:

bashCopy code

```
kubectl create deployment my-app --image=my-app-image --replicas=3
```

This command creates a Kubernetes deployment named "my-app" with three replicas of the "my-app-image" container image, ensuring redundancy and fault tolerance. Data redundancy involves maintaining multiple copies of data across different storage devices or locations to ensure data availability and integrity. Replication techniques such as master-slave replication, multi-master replication, and sharding are commonly used to replicate data across distributed databases and storage systems. For example, in MySQL, administrators can configure master-slave replication to replicate data changes from a master database server to one or more slave servers:

bashCopy code

```
CHANGE MASTER TO MASTER_HOST='master_host',
MASTER_USER='replication_user',
MASTER_PASSWORD='password',
MASTER_LOG_FILE='binlog_file',
MASTER_LOG_POS=binlog_position; START SLAVE;
```

These commands configure the slave server to replicate data changes from the master server and start the replication process.

Checkpointing is a technique used in distributed systems and parallel processing to save the state of computations periodically, allowing them to be restarted from the last checkpoint in case of failures. Checkpointing helps minimize the amount of work lost in the event of failures and ensures progress is not lost. For example, in Apache Spark, a distributed data processing framework, developers can configure checkpointing to save the state of RDDs (Resilient Distributed Datasets) to durable storage:

pythonCopy code

```
from pyspark import SparkContext sc = SparkContext("local", "CheckpointExample") sc.setCheckpointDir("/tmp/spark-checkpoint") rdd = sc.parallelize(range(1000)) rdd.checkpoint()
```

This Python code creates a SparkContext with local execution mode and sets the checkpoint directory to "/tmp/spark-checkpoint". It then parallelizes a range of numbers into an RDD and checkpoints the RDD, saving its state to durable storage.

In summary, error handling and failure recovery mechanisms are essential components of software and system design, designed to detect, respond to, and recover from errors and failures gracefully. By employing techniques such as exception handling, retries, timeouts, redundancy, replication, and checkpointing, developers and system administrators can ensure that systems remain operational, reliable, and resilient, even in the face of unexpected events. These mechanisms play a crucial role in maintaining system stability, availability, and performance, ultimately enhancing the user experience and minimizing disruptions.

Chapter 6: Essential Tools for Data-Intensive Applications

Database Management Systems (DBMS) are essential software tools used for storing, managing, and retrieving data efficiently. They serve as the backbone of modern applications and are crucial for organizing and maintaining structured information. DBMSes provide a structured way to interact with data, allowing users to perform various operations such as inserting, updating, querying, and deleting data. These systems offer several advantages over traditional file-based data storage methods, including data integrity, concurrency control, security, and scalability. One of the most widely used types of DBMS is the relational database management system (RDBMS), which organizes data into tables consisting of rows and columns. SQL (Structured Query Language) is the standard language used to interact with relational databases, allowing users to perform operations such as creating tables, inserting data, and querying data. For example, to create a new table named "employees" in a MySQL database, users can execute the following SQL command: sqlCopy code
CREATE TABLE employees (id INT PRIMARY KEY, name VARCHAR(50), age INT, department VARCHAR(50));
This SQL command creates a table named "employees" with columns for employee ID, name, age, and department.
In addition to relational databases, there are also other types of DBMSes, such as NoSQL databases, which are designed to handle unstructured or semi-structured data

and offer flexible data models. NoSQL databases use different data models, such as document-oriented, key-value, column-family, and graph databases, to accommodate diverse data types and access patterns. For example, MongoDB is a popular document-oriented NoSQL database that stores data in JSON-like documents and allows for flexible schema design. To insert a document into a MongoDB collection using the MongoDB shell, users can execute the following command:

bashCopy code

```
mongo
```

This command opens the MongoDB shell, where users can interact with the database. To insert a document into a collection named "employees", users can execute the following JavaScript command:

javascriptCopy code

```
db.employees.insertOne({ name: "John Doe", age: 30, department: "IT" });
```

This command inserts a document representing an employee into the "employees" collection.

Another type of DBMS is the column-family database, which stores data in columns rather than rows and is optimized for analytical queries and aggregations. Apache Cassandra is a popular column-family NoSQL database known for its high availability, fault tolerance, and linear scalability. To create a new keyspace (database) and table in Apache Cassandra using the cqlsh (Cassandra Query Language Shell), users can execute the following commands:

bashCopy code

```
cqlsh
```

This command opens the cqlsh shell, where users can execute CQL commands. To create a new keyspace named "example" and a table named "employees" within that keyspace, users can execute the following CQL commands:
cql|Copy code

CREATE KEYSPACE example WITH replication = {'class': 'SimpleStrategy', 'replication_factor': 1};

This command creates a new keyspace named "example" with a replication factor of 1.
cql|Copy code

USE example;

This command switches to the "example" keyspace.
cql|Copy code

CREATE TABLE employees (id INT PRIMARY KEY, name TEXT, age INT, department TEXT);

This command creates a new table named "employees" with columns for employee ID, name, age, and department.

Once the table is created, users can insert data into the table using CQL insert statements.

Aside from relational and NoSQL databases, there are also in-memory databases that store data primarily in RAM, offering fast read and write access. These databases are often used for caching, real-time analytics, and high-performance applications. Redis is a popular in-memory data store known for its speed, simplicity, and support for advanced data structures such as strings, lists, sets, and sorted sets. To set a value in Redis using the redis-cli (Redis Command Line Interface), users can execute the following command:
bash|Copy code

redis-cli

This command opens the redis-cli shell, where users can interact with the Redis server. To set a key named "name" with the value "John Doe", users can execute the following command:

bashCopy code

```
SET name "John Doe"
```

This command sets the value of the "name" key to "John Doe" in the Redis server.

Database Management Systems play a crucial role in modern applications, providing efficient and reliable storage solutions for managing structured, semi-structured, and unstructured data. By leveraging different types of DBMSes, developers and organizations can build scalable, performant, and resilient systems that meet the diverse needs of their applications. Whether using relational databases for transactional data, NoSQL databases for flexible data models, column-family databases for analytical queries, or in-memory databases for high-speed caching, selecting the right DBMS is essential for achieving optimal performance, scalability, and reliability. As technology continues to evolve, new types of DBMSes and innovative storage solutions will continue to emerge, offering developers and organizations even more options for building robust and scalable applications.

Chapter 7: Security Considerations in Application Design

Data visualization tools are essential software applications used for creating graphical representations of data to facilitate analysis, exploration, and communication of insights. These tools play a crucial role in transforming raw data into meaningful visualizations, enabling users to uncover patterns, trends, and relationships that may not be apparent in raw data alone. Data visualization tools are widely used across various industries and domains, including business intelligence, data analytics, scientific research, and data journalism, to make data-driven decisions and convey complex information effectively.

One of the most popular data visualization tools is Tableau, which offers a powerful suite of features for creating interactive and visually appealing dashboards, reports, and charts. Tableau Desktop is the primary tool used for creating visualizations, allowing users to connect to various data sources, import data, and create visualizations using a drag-and-drop interface. To create a basic bar chart in Tableau Desktop, users can follow these steps:

Connect to a data source: Users can connect to a data source such as Excel, CSV, or a database by selecting the appropriate connector and providing connection details.

bashCopy code

```
# Example CLI command to connect to a CSV file in Tableau Desktop tableau connect-to-file data.csv
```

Import data: Once connected to a data source, users can import data into Tableau by selecting the desired tables or sheets and dragging them onto the canvas.

bashCopy code

Example CLI command to import data from a CSV file in Tableau Desktop tableau import-data data.csv

Create a bar chart: To create a bar chart, users can drag the desired dimension (e.g., product category) to the Columns shelf and the measure (e.g., sales revenue) to the Rows shelf. Tableau automatically generates a bar chart based on the selected dimensions and measures.

bashCopy code

Example CLI command to create a bar chart in Tableau Desktop tableau create-bar-chart --dimension=product_category --measure=sales_revenue

Another popular data visualization tool is Microsoft Power BI, which offers a comprehensive suite of features for data analysis, visualization, and collaboration. Power BI Desktop is the primary tool used for creating visualizations, allowing users to connect to data sources, transform data, and create interactive reports and dashboards. To create a simple line chart in Power BI Desktop, users can follow these steps:

Connect to a data source: Users can connect to a data source such as Excel, SQL Server, or a web service by selecting the appropriate connector and providing connection details.

bashCopy code

Example CLI command to connect to a SQL Server database in Power BI Desktop powerbi connect-to-

database --server=servername --database=databasename --username=username --password=password

Import data: Once connected to a data source, users can import data into Power BI by selecting the desired tables or views and loading them into the data model.

bashCopy code

```
# Example CLI command to import data from a SQL Server database in Power BI Desktop powerbi import-data --tables=tablename1,tablename2
```

Create a line chart: To create a line chart, users can drag the desired date or time dimension (e.g., date) to the Axis field well and the measure (e.g., sales revenue) to the Values field well. Power BI automatically generates a line chart based on the selected dimensions and measures.

bashCopy code

```
# Example CLI command to create a line chart in Power BI Desktop powerbi create-line-chart --dimension=date --measure=sales_revenue
```

In addition to Tableau and Power BI, there are also open-source data visualization tools such as Matplotlib and Seaborn, which are widely used in the Python ecosystem for creating static and interactive visualizations. Matplotlib is a versatile plotting library that allows users to create a wide range of visualizations, including line plots, bar charts, histograms, scatter plots, and more. To create a basic line plot in Matplotlib, users can execute the following Python script:

pythonCopy code

```
import matplotlib.pyplot as plt # Sample data x = [1, 2, 3, 4, 5] y = [10, 20, 15, 25, 30] # Create a line plot
```

```
plt.plot(x, y) plt.xlabel('X-axis') plt.ylabel('Y-axis')
plt.title('Line Plot') plt.show()
```

This Python script generates a simple line plot using Matplotlib, with the x-axis representing the data points and the y-axis representing the corresponding values.

Seaborn is another Python library built on top of Matplotlib, offering additional functionality and higher-level interfaces for creating statistical visualizations. Seaborn provides support for visualizing statistical relationships, categorical data, distributions, and more. To create a basic scatter plot in Seaborn, users can execute the following Python script:

```
pythonCopy code
import seaborn as sns import matplotlib.pyplot as plt #
Sample data x = [1, 2, 3, 4, 5] y = [10, 20, 15, 25, 30]
# Create a scatter plot sns.scatterplot(x=x, y=y)
plt.xlabel('X-axis') plt.ylabel('Y-axis') plt.title('Scatter
Plot') plt.show()
```

This Python script generates a simple scatter plot using Seaborn, visualizing the relationship between two variables (x and y).

In summary, data visualization tools are essential for transforming raw data into meaningful visualizations, enabling users to analyze data effectively and communicate insights clearly. Whether using commercial tools like Tableau and Power BI or open-source libraries like Matplotlib and Seaborn, selecting the right data visualization tool depends on factors such as the specific requirements of the project, the skill set of the users, and the available budget. By leveraging data visualization tools, organizations can unlock the full potential of their data and make informed decisions that drive business success.

Authentication and authorization mechanisms are fundamental components of security systems, crucial for controlling access to resources and ensuring the confidentiality, integrity, and availability of sensitive information. Authentication verifies the identity of users or entities attempting to access a system or application, while authorization determines what actions or resources a user is allowed to access based on their authenticated identity and assigned permissions. These mechanisms are essential for protecting against unauthorized access, data breaches, and other security threats, and are widely used across various domains, including information technology, cybersecurity, and digital identity management.

One of the most common authentication mechanisms is username and password authentication, where users provide a unique username and a secret password to access a system or application. This mechanism is widely used in web applications, email services, and operating systems to verify the identity of users. For example, to authenticate a user using the command line in a Linux environment, administrators can use the "passwd" command to set or change a user's password:

bashCopy code

```
passwd username
```

This command prompts the administrator to enter and confirm a new password for the specified username.

Another widely used authentication mechanism is multi-factor authentication (MFA), which requires users to provide multiple forms of identification to access a system or application. MFA typically combines something the user knows (e.g., a password) with something they have (e.g., a mobile device or security token) or something they are (e.g., biometric data such as fingerprints or facial recognition). This additional layer of security enhances protection against unauthorized access, even if a user's password is compromised. For example, popular authentication services like Google Authenticator and Microsoft Authenticator provide time-based one-time passwords (TOTPs) that users must enter in addition to their passwords when logging in. To set up multi-factor authentication using Google Authenticator, users can follow these steps:

Install the Google Authenticator app on a mobile device.

Log in to the account or service requiring multi-factor authentication.

Enable multi-factor authentication and select the option to use an authenticator app.

Scan the QR code displayed on the screen using the Google Authenticator app.

Enter the TOTP generated by the app to verify and complete the setup.

Once set up, users will be prompted to enter the TOTP generated by the Google Authenticator app in addition to their password when logging in.

In addition to authentication, authorization mechanisms control access to resources and functionalities based on the authenticated identity of users. Role-based access control (RBAC) is a commonly used authorization model that assigns permissions to users based on their roles within an organization. Users are assigned roles that define their access rights, and permissions are granted or revoked based on those roles. For example, in a web application, users may be assigned roles such as "admin," "editor," or "viewer," with corresponding permissions to create, edit, or view content. To manage roles and permissions in a web application using a command-line interface, developers can use frameworks like Django, which provide built-in support for RBAC. To create a new role in a Django application, developers can use the "manage.py" command-line utility:

bashCopy code

```
python manage.py create_role admin
```

This command creates a new role named "admin" in the Django application.

To grant permissions to the "admin" role, developers can use the Django admin interface or the command-line interface:

bashCopy code

```
python manage.py grant_permission admin create_content
```

This command grants the "create_content" permission to the "admin" role, allowing users with the "admin" role to create content in the application.

Attribute-based access control (ABAC) is another authorization model that grants access based on the attributes associated with users, resources, and environmental conditions. ABAC policies evaluate attributes such as user roles, department, location, time of day, and device type to determine access rights dynamically. This flexible model allows organizations to implement fine-grained access control based on specific attributes and conditions. To implement ABAC policies in an application using a command-line interface, developers can use policy management tools like Open Policy Agent (OPA), which provides a declarative language called Rego for writing policy rules. For example, to define an ABAC policy that grants access to users in the "admin" role during business hours, developers can write a Rego policy rule:

regoCopy code

package authz default allow = false allow { input.role == "admin" is_business_hours } is_business_hours { time.now.hour >= 9 time.now.hour < 17 }

This Rego policy rule grants access to users with the "admin" role during business hours (9:00 AM to 5:00 PM).

OAuth (Open Authorization) is a widely used authentication and authorization protocol that allows users to grant third-party applications access to their resources without sharing their credentials directly. OAuth enables secure authorization flows between different services, such as social media platforms, APIs, and mobile applications. To implement OAuth authentication in a web application using a command-line interface, developers can use OAuth libraries and frameworks like OAuthLib for Python. To authenticate users using OAuth 2.0 in a Django application, developers can use the "django-oauth-toolkit" library, which provides built-in support for OAuth 2.0. To install the library, developers can use the following pip command:

bashCopy code

pip install django-oauth-toolkit

Once installed, developers can configure OAuth 2.0 authentication using the Django settings and URL routing. They can define OAuth 2.0 scopes, client applications, and authorization endpoints in the Django application settings.

To define OAuth 2.0 scopes, developers can add the following configuration to the Django settings:

pythonCopy code

```
OAUTH2_PROVIDER = { 'SCOPES': {'read': 'Read scope', 'write': 'Write scope'}, }
```

This configuration defines two OAuth 2.0 scopes named "read" and "write" with corresponding descriptions.

To define OAuth 2.0 client applications, developers can use the Django admin interface or the command-line interface:

bashCopy code

```
python manage.py create_application --name "MyApp" --client-type confidential --authorization-grant-type authorization-code --redirect-uris "https://example.com/callback"
```

This command creates a new OAuth 2.0 client application named "MyApp" with confidential client type, authorization code grant type, and redirect URI "https://example.com/callback".

To define OAuth 2.0 authorization endpoints, developers can add URL routing configurations to the Django application:

pythonCopy code

```
from oauth2_provider.views import AuthorizationView
urlpatterns = [ ... path('oauth/authorize/', AuthorizationView.as_view(), name='authorize'), ... ]
```

This URL routing configuration defines an OAuth 2.0 authorization endpoint at "/oauth/authorize/".

Once configured, users can authenticate using OAuth 2.0 by redirecting to the authorization endpoint and granting permissions to the client application. The authorization server then issues access tokens to the client application, allowing it to access protected resources on behalf of the user.

In summary, authentication and authorization mechanisms are essential components of security systems, crucial for controlling access to resources and protecting against unauthorized access and security threats. Whether using traditional authentication methods like username and password, multi-factor authentication, role-based access control, attribute-based access control, or OAuth, selecting the right mechanisms depends on factors such as the security requirements of the application, user experience considerations, and compliance with industry regulations. By implementing robust authentication and authorization mechanisms, organizations can ensure the security and integrity of their systems and data, safeguarding against unauthorized access and potential security breaches.

Chapter 8: Performance Optimization Techniques

Caching strategies are essential techniques used in software development to improve the performance and efficiency of applications by storing frequently accessed data in temporary storage. Caching plays a crucial role in reducing latency, network traffic, and resource consumption, ultimately enhancing the overall user experience. By caching data closer to the point of use, applications can retrieve information more quickly, reduce load on backend systems, and handle higher volumes of traffic more efficiently. There are various caching strategies and techniques available, each suited to different use cases and scenarios, including in-memory caching, browser caching, content delivery networks (CDNs), and database caching.

One of the most common caching strategies is in-memory caching, which involves storing data in the main memory (RAM) of a server or application. In-memory caching is extremely fast, as data can be retrieved directly from memory without needing to access disk storage or external systems. This caching strategy is often used for caching frequently accessed data such as database query results, session data, and computed values. To implement in-memory caching in a web application using a command-line interface, developers can use caching libraries and frameworks like Redis or Memcached. For example, to set up caching with Redis, developers can install the Redis server and client libraries using package managers such as apt or yum:

bashCopy code

sudo apt-get install redis-server

Once installed, developers can configure the application to use Redis as a caching backend by specifying the Redis server address and port in the application settings.

Another caching strategy is browser caching, which involves storing static assets such as images, CSS files, and JavaScript files in the local cache of web browsers. Browser caching reduces the need for repeated downloads of static resources and improves page load times for subsequent visits. Web developers can control browser caching behavior using HTTP cache headers such as Cache-Control, Expires, and Last-Modified. To configure browser caching for static assets in a web application, developers can use server configuration files such as .htaccess for Apache or nginx.conf for Nginx. For example, to set an expiration time of one year for static assets in Apache, developers can add the following directives to the .htaccess file:

apacheCopy code

<IfModule mod_expires.c> ExpiresActive On ExpiresByType text/css "access plus 1 year" ExpiresByType application/javascript "access plus 1 year" ExpiresByType image/jpeg "access plus 1 year" ExpiresByType image/png "access plus 1 year" </IfModule>

This configuration sets an expiration time of one year for CSS, JavaScript, JPEG, and PNG files, instructing web browsers to cache these resources for faster subsequent access.

Content delivery networks (CDNs) are another caching strategy used to improve the performance and availability of web applications by distributing content across a network of geographically distributed servers. CDNs cache static assets such as images, videos, and documents on edge servers located closer to end users, reducing latency and network congestion. To deploy a CDN for a web application, developers can use CDN providers such as Cloudflare, Akamai, or Amazon CloudFront. After signing up for a CDN service, developers can configure the CDN settings and point the application's domain to the CDN's edge servers using DNS configuration. This allows the CDN to cache and serve static assets from the closest edge server to the end users, improving performance and reliability.

Database caching is another caching strategy used to improve the performance of database-driven applications by caching query results, frequently accessed data, and computed values in memory or disk storage. Database caching reduces the need for repeated database queries and improves response times for database-driven operations. Many modern relational database management systems (RDBMS) and NoSQL databases provide built-in caching mechanisms and query caching features to optimize performance. For example, in MySQL, developers can enable query caching by setting the "query_cache_type" and "query_cache_size" parameters in the MySQL configuration file (my.cnf):

bashCopy code

[mysqld] query_cache_type = 1 query_cache_size = 64M

This configuration enables query caching and allocates 64 megabytes of memory for storing cached query results.

Furthermore, developers can implement custom caching strategies and techniques tailored to the specific requirements and characteristics of their applications. For instance, they can use cache invalidation techniques such as time-based expiration, event-driven invalidation, or manual invalidation to ensure the cache remains up-to-date and consistent with the underlying data source. Additionally, developers can implement cache warming techniques to pre-load or populate caches with frequently accessed data during application startup or idle periods, reducing cache miss rates and improving overall performance.

In summary, caching strategies are essential techniques used to improve the performance, scalability, and efficiency of applications by storing frequently accessed data in temporary storage. By leveraging caching mechanisms such as in-memory caching, browser caching, CDNs, and database caching, developers can reduce latency, minimize network traffic, and enhance the overall user experience. With a thorough understanding of caching strategies and techniques, developers can optimize the performance of their applications and ensure they deliver fast, responsive, and reliable user experiences.

Query optimization methods are crucial techniques used in database management systems to enhance the performance and efficiency of queries executed against large datasets. These methods aim to minimize the query execution time, reduce resource consumption, and improve overall system throughput by optimizing query execution plans, access paths, and data retrieval strategies. In a relational database management system (RDBMS), query optimization plays a significant role in ensuring fast and efficient data retrieval operations, particularly in scenarios involving complex queries, joins, aggregations, and data manipulation tasks. There are various query optimization methods and strategies employed by database systems to achieve optimal query performance, including indexing, query rewriting, statistics collection, query plan analysis, and algorithm selection.

One of the most fundamental query optimization techniques is indexing, which involves creating and maintaining data structures known as indexes to accelerate data retrieval operations. Indexes provide fast access paths to data by organizing and storing key columns in sorted order, allowing the database system to quickly locate and retrieve rows that satisfy the query predicates. Common types of indexes include B-tree indexes, hash indexes, and bitmap indexes, each suited to different data access patterns and query types. To optimize query performance using indexing, database administrators can create indexes on columns frequently used in query predicates, join conditions, and order by clauses. For example, to create an index on the "name" column of a table named "employees" in PostgreSQL, administrators can use the following SQL command:

sqlCopy code

```
CREATE INDEX idx_name ON employees (name);
```

This command creates a B-tree index named "idx_name" on the "name" column of the "employees" table, allowing the database system to quickly locate rows by name.

Another query optimization method is query rewriting, which involves transforming a given query into an equivalent but more efficient form to improve execution performance. Query rewriting techniques include query normalization, query simplification, and query expansion, each aimed at optimizing query syntax, semantics, and execution semantics. Database systems use query rewriting to eliminate redundant or unnecessary operations, rewrite suboptimal query plans, and enforce query optimization rules. To perform query rewriting in a database system, developers can use query optimization tools and frameworks provided by database vendors or third-party software vendors. For example, in Oracle Database, developers can use the Query Optimizer tool to analyze query execution plans, identify performance bottlenecks, and suggest query rewriting strategies to improve performance.

Statistics collection is another essential query optimization method used to gather and maintain statistical information about database objects such as tables, columns, and indexes. Statistics provide valuable insights into the data distribution, cardinality, and selectivity of query predicates, helping the query optimizer make informed decisions about query execution plans and access paths. Database systems collect statistics using sampling techniques, histogram analysis, and data profiling algorithms to estimate the size and distribution of data objects accurately. To collect statistics on a table in SQL Server, administrators can use the following Transact-SQL (T-SQL) command:

sqlCopy code

UPDATE STATISTICS table_name;

This command updates statistics for all columns in the specified table, allowing the query optimizer to make more accurate cost estimates and choose optimal query execution plans.

Query plan analysis is another crucial query optimization method used to analyze and optimize query execution plans generated by the query optimizer. Query plans represent the sequence of operations performed by the database system to execute a given query, including table scans, index scans, join operations, and sorting operations. Database administrators use query plan analysis tools and utilities to examine query plans, identify performance bottlenecks, and tune query execution strategies. For example, in MySQL, developers can use the EXPLAIN statement to analyze query execution plans and understand how the database system processes queries:

sqlCopy code

```
EXPLAIN SELECT * FROM employees WHERE department_id = 100;
```

This command displays the query execution plan for the specified SQL query, showing the execution order, access methods, and estimated costs associated with each operation.

Algorithm selection is another query optimization method used to choose the most efficient algorithms and data structures for query processing and data retrieval tasks. Database systems employ a variety of algorithms for query evaluation, join processing, sorting, grouping, and aggregation, each with different performance characteristics and trade-offs. The query optimizer evaluates candidate algorithms based on factors such as data distribution, query complexity, and available system resources to select the most suitable algorithm for each query. For example, in PostgreSQL, developers can configure the query planner to use specific join algorithms such as nested loop joins, hash joins, or merge joins based on query hints or optimizer parameters:

sqlCopy code

```
SET enable_nestloop TO off;
```

This command disables nested loop joins in the PostgreSQL query planner, instructing the optimizer to use alternative join algorithms for query processing.

In summary, query optimization methods are essential techniques used in database management systems to improve the performance and efficiency of query execution operations. By employing indexing, query rewriting, statistics collection, query plan analysis, and algorithm selection, database systems can optimize query execution plans, access paths, and data retrieval strategies to achieve optimal performance. With a thorough understanding of query optimization techniques and best practices, database administrators and developers can fine-tune database systems, enhance application performance, and deliver fast and responsive user experiences.

Chapter 9: Integration Strategies for Data-Intensive Systems

API integration techniques are essential methodologies used in software development to facilitate communication and data exchange between different applications, systems, or services via Application Programming Interfaces (APIs). These techniques enable seamless integration and interoperability between disparate systems, allowing them to exchange data, trigger actions, and collaborate effectively. API integration is a fundamental aspect of modern software architecture, enabling developers to leverage external services, libraries, and platforms to enhance the functionality, scalability, and extensibility of their applications. There are various API integration techniques and patterns available, each suited to different use cases, requirements, and integration scenarios, including synchronous and asynchronous integration, RESTful APIs, GraphQL, Webhooks, and messaging protocols such as MQTT and AMQP.

One of the most common API integration techniques is synchronous integration, where applications communicate with each other in real-time by making synchronous HTTP requests and receiving immediate responses. Synchronous integration is well-suited for scenarios where immediate response times are essential, such as user-facing applications, web services, and interactive interfaces. To implement synchronous integration with a RESTful API using a command-line interface, developers can use tools like cURL or HTTPie to send HTTP requests and receive responses. For example, to make a GET request to a RESTful API endpoint using cURL, developers can use the following command:

bashCopy code

```
curl -X GET https://api.example.com/resource
```

This command sends a GET request to the specified API endpoint and prints the response to the command line.

Another API integration technique is asynchronous integration, where applications communicate with each other asynchronously by exchanging messages or events without requiring an immediate response. Asynchronous integration is suitable for scenarios where decoupling, scalability, and fault tolerance are critical, such as event-driven architectures, message queues, and distributed systems. To implement asynchronous integration with a message queue using a command-line interface, developers can use messaging protocols such as Advanced Message Queuing Protocol (AMQP) or Message Queuing Telemetry Transport (MQTT). For example, to publish a message to an MQTT broker using the mosquitto_pub command-line utility, developers can use the following command:

bashCopy code

```
mosquitto_pub -h broker.example.com -t topic -m "Hello, World!"
```

This command publishes a message with the content "Hello, World!" to the specified MQTT topic on the MQTT broker.

RESTful APIs are another widely used API integration technique that follows the principles of Representational State Transfer (REST) and uses standard HTTP methods such as GET, POST, PUT, and DELETE for communication. RESTful APIs provide a uniform interface for interacting with resources over the web and are commonly used for building web services, microservices, and distributed systems. To integrate with a RESTful API using a command-line interface, developers can use HTTP client libraries and frameworks such as axios for Node.js or requests for Python. For example, to make a POST request to a RESTful API endpoint using the axios library in Node.js, developers can use the following code:

javascriptCopy code

```
const axios = require('axios');
axios.post('https://api.example.com/resource', { data: 'example data' }) .then(response => { console.log(response.data); }) .catch(error => { console.error(error); });
```

This code sends a POST request to the specified RESTful API endpoint with the provided data and logs the response to the console.

GraphQL is another API integration technique that allows clients to query and manipulate data using a flexible and efficient query language. Unlike RESTful APIs, which expose predefined endpoints for accessing resources, GraphQL APIs enable clients to specify the shape and structure of the data they require using a single HTTP endpoint. To integrate with a GraphQL API using a command-line interface, developers can use GraphQL client libraries and tools such as Apollo Client or GraphQL Request. For example, to execute a GraphQL query against a GraphQL API endpoint using the curl command-line utility, developers can use the following command:

bashCopy code

```
curl -X POST -H "Content-Type: application/json" -d '{"query": "{ hello }"}' https://api.example.com/graphql
```

This command sends a GraphQL query to the specified GraphQL API endpoint and prints the response to the command line.

Webhooks are another API integration technique used to enable real-time communication between applications by allowing one application to notify another application of events or updates via HTTP callbacks. Webhooks are commonly used for event-driven integration scenarios such as notifying external systems of new data, triggering automated workflows, and integrating with third-party services. To implement webhooks using a command-line interface, developers can use webhook server libraries and frameworks such as Express.js for Node.js or Flask for Python. For example, to create a webhook endpoint in a Node.js application using Express.js, developers can use the following code:

javascriptCopy code

```
const express = require('express'); const bodyParser = require('body-parser'); const app = express(); app.use(bodyParser.json()); app.post('/webhook',
```

```
(req, res) => { console.log('Webhook received:',
req.body); res.sendStatus(200); }); app.listen(3000, ()
=> { console.log('Webhook server listening on port
3000'); });
```

This code creates a webhook endpoint at the "/webhook" URL path that logs incoming webhook payloads and responds with a 200 OK status code.

In summary, API integration techniques are essential methodologies used in software development to facilitate communication and data exchange between different applications, systems, or services. By leveraging synchronous and asynchronous integration, RESTful APIs, GraphQL, Webhooks, and messaging protocols, developers can build scalable, interoperable, and efficient systems that meet the diverse integration requirements of modern applications. With a solid understanding of API integration techniques and best practices, developers can design robust and flexible architectures, streamline development workflows, and deliver seamless user experiences across diverse platforms and environments.

ETL (Extract, Transform, Load) processes are fundamental procedures in data warehousing and business intelligence, facilitating the extraction, transformation, and loading of data from various sources into a centralized repository for analysis and reporting. These processes are vital for organizations to gather, consolidate, and analyze data from disparate sources, enabling informed decision-making and strategic planning. ETL processes involve extracting raw data from source systems, transforming it into a consistent and structured format, and loading it into a target database or data warehouse for analysis. The extraction phase retrieves data from multiple sources such as databases, files, APIs, and cloud services, while the transformation phase applies various data manipulation and cleansing operations to ensure data quality and consistency. Finally, the load phase loads the transformed data into a target database or data warehouse, ready for analysis and reporting.

The first step in an ETL process is extraction, which involves retrieving data from one or more source systems. Source systems may include relational databases, flat files, web services, APIs, cloud storage, and streaming data sources. To extract data from relational databases, developers can use SQL queries or database management tools such as MySQL Workbench or pgAdmin. For example, to extract data from a MySQL database using the command line, developers can use the "mysqldump" command:

bashCopy code

```
mysqldump -u username -p database_name > data_dump.sql
```

This command exports the contents of the specified database to a SQL file named "data_dump.sql", including table structures and data.

For extracting data from flat files such as CSV or JSON files, developers can use command-line utilities like "cat", "awk", or "jq". For instance, to extract data from a CSV file using the command line, developers can use the "cat" command to display the contents of the file:

```bash
cat data.csv
```

This command outputs the contents of the CSV file to the terminal, which can then be processed further using other command-line tools or scripts.

After extraction, the next step in the ETL process is transformation, where the extracted data undergoes various cleansing, validation, and enrichment operations to ensure consistency and quality. Transformation tasks may include data type conversion, null value handling, duplicate removal, data deduplication, and data standardization. To perform data transformation tasks, developers can use scripting languages like Python, Perl, or shell scripting, along with libraries and frameworks such as pandas, NumPy, or Apache Spark. For example, to perform data transformation tasks using Python and pandas, developers can write scripts to read data from source files, apply transformation functions, and write transformed data to target files. Here's a simple example using Python and pandas:

```python
import pandas as pd # Read data from CSV file data =
pd.read_csv('data.csv') # Perform data transformation
# Example: Convert column values to uppercase
data['Name'] = data['Name'].str.upper() # Write
transformed data to CSV file
data.to_csv('transformed_data.csv', index=False)
```

This Python script reads data from a CSV file, converts the values in the "Name" column to uppercase, and writes the transformed data to another CSV file named "transformed_data.csv".

Finally, after data extraction and transformation, the last step in the ETL process is loading, where the transformed data is loaded into a target database or data warehouse for storage and analysis. Target systems may include relational databases, data lakes, data warehouses, or cloud-based storage solutions. To load data into a target database, developers can use SQL statements or database-specific utilities such as "LOAD DATA INFILE" in MySQL or "COPY" in PostgreSQL.

For example, to load data into a MySQL database using the command line, developers can use the "mysql" command-line client:

bashCopy code

```
mysql -u username -p database_name < data_dump.sql
```

This command imports the contents of the SQL file generated during the extraction phase into the specified MySQL database.

For loading data into a data warehouse or cloud storage solution, developers can use ETL tools and platforms such as Apache Airflow, Talend, Informatica, or Amazon Redshift's COPY command. These tools provide graphical user interfaces (GUIs) or command-line interfaces (CLIs) for designing ETL workflows, scheduling data pipelines, and orchestrating data movement tasks. For example, to load data into Amazon Redshift using the AWS Command Line Interface (CLI), developers can use the "copy" command:

bashCopy code

```
aws redshift copy from 's3://bucket-name/file-path'
credentials
'aws_access_key_id=YOUR_ACCESS_KEY;aws_secret_ac
cess_key=YOUR_SECRET_KEY' delimiter ',' region 'us-
west-2';
```

This command copies data from an Amazon S3 bucket to an Amazon Redshift table, specifying the credentials and other parameters required for authentication and data transfer.

In summary, ETL (Extract, Transform, Load) processes are essential procedures in data warehousing and business intelligence, enabling organizations to extract, transform, and load data from diverse sources into centralized repositories for analysis and reporting. By employing command-line utilities, scripting languages, database management tools, and ETL platforms, developers can design, deploy, and manage ETL workflows to streamline data integration tasks and support informed decision-making processes. With proper planning and execution, ETL processes can ensure data quality, consistency, and availability, empowering organizations to derive valuable insights and drive business growth.

Chapter 10: Future Trends in Application Design

Edge computing and IoT integration have emerged as critical components in modern computing architectures, revolutionizing how data is processed, analyzed, and acted upon at the network's edge. These technologies are reshaping various industries, from manufacturing and healthcare to transportation and smart cities, by enabling real-time decision-making, reducing latency, and enhancing operational efficiency. Edge computing refers to the practice of processing data closer to the source of generation, often at or near the edge of the network, rather than relying on centralized cloud infrastructure. It leverages distributed computing resources, including edge devices, gateways, and edge servers, to perform computation, storage, and analytics tasks locally, thus minimizing data transmission latency and bandwidth consumption. IoT (Internet of Things), on the other hand, encompasses a network of interconnected devices equipped with sensors, actuators, and communication capabilities, enabling them to collect, exchange, and analyze data autonomously. By integrating edge computing with IoT technologies, organizations can unlock new opportunities for real-time data processing, predictive analytics, and intelligent decision-making at the edge of the network.

The integration of edge computing and IoT technologies presents numerous benefits for organizations seeking to harness the power of real-time data analytics and automation. One of the key advantages is reduced latency, as edge computing enables data processing and analysis to occur closer to the point of data generation. This is particularly important for applications that require immediate response times, such as industrial automation, autonomous vehicles, and healthcare monitoring systems. By processing data locally at the edge, organizations can minimize the delay associated with transmitting data to centralized cloud servers, thereby improving system responsiveness and user experience. To deploy edge computing infrastructure, organizations can leverage edge computing platforms and frameworks such as AWS IoT Greengrass, Microsoft Azure IoT Edge, or Google Cloud IoT Edge. These platforms enable organizations to deploy and manage edge computing workloads on edge devices and gateways seamlessly. For example, to deploy an edge computing application using AWS IoT Greengrass, organizations can use the AWS Command Line Interface (CLI) to create and configure Greengrass groups, which represent collections of edge devices and associated resources:

bashCopy code

```
aws greengrass create-group --name my-greengrass-group
```

This command creates a new Greengrass group named "my-greengrass-group" in the AWS IoT Greengrass service. Another benefit of edge computing and IoT integration is improved scalability and reliability. By distributing computing resources and processing tasks across edge devices and gateways, organizations can achieve greater scalability and fault tolerance in their IoT deployments. Edge computing allows organizations to offload computational tasks from centralized servers to edge nodes, reducing the burden on cloud infrastructure and enabling more efficient resource utilization. Additionally, edge computing enables organizations to operate in disconnected or low-bandwidth environments, where continuous connectivity to centralized cloud servers may be unreliable or impractical. Edge devices can cache data locally and perform computation autonomously, ensuring continuity of operations even in adverse network conditions.

Furthermore, the integration of edge computing and IoT technologies enables organizations to implement real-time analytics and machine learning at the edge, allowing them to derive actionable insights from streaming data sources. Edge devices can preprocess sensor data, detect anomalies, and trigger automated responses locally, without relying on centralized cloud services. This capability is particularly valuable for applications requiring low-latency decision-making, such as predictive maintenance, asset tracking, and real-time monitoring. To deploy machine learning models at the edge, organizations can use edge computing frameworks that support model deployment and inference on edge devices. For example, TensorFlow Lite for Microcontrollers is a lightweight machine learning framework designed for microcontroller-based edge devices, enabling organizations to deploy and execute machine learning models directly on IoT devices:

bashCopy code

pip install tensorflow

This command installs the TensorFlow library, including TensorFlow Lite for Microcontrollers, on the local development environment.

Another example is AWS IoT Greengrass ML Inference, a feature of AWS IoT Greengrass that enables organizations to deploy machine learning models to edge devices and perform inference locally:

bashCopy code

```
aws greengrass create-machine-learning-model --name
my-model                                    --role-arn
arn:aws:iam::123456789012:role/service-
role/MyGreengrassRole
```

This command creates a new machine learning model in the AWS IoT Greengrass service, specifying the IAM role required for model deployment and execution.

In addition to real-time analytics and machine learning, edge computing and IoT integration enable organizations to enhance data privacy and security by processing sensitive data locally and minimizing data exposure to external networks. Edge devices can encrypt data at rest and in transit, implement access controls and authentication mechanisms, and enforce data residency requirements, thereby reducing the risk of data breaches and unauthorized access. By keeping sensitive data within the confines of the local network, organizations can maintain greater control over their data and comply with regulatory requirements such as GDPR (General Data Protection Regulation) and HIPAA (Health Insurance Portability and Accountability Act).

In summary, the integration of edge computing and IoT technologies offers numerous benefits for organizations seeking to leverage real-time data processing, analytics, and automation at the network edge. By deploying edge computing infrastructure and IoT devices, organizations can reduce latency, improve scalability, and enhance reliability in their IoT deployments. Furthermore, edge computing enables organizations to implement real-time analytics, machine learning, and security mechanisms locally, thereby empowering them to derive actionable insights, enhance operational efficiency, and protect sensitive data. With the continued advancement of edge computing and IoT technologies, organizations have unprecedented opportunities to innovate and transform their business operations, driving value creation and competitive advantage in the digital age.

AI and machine learning applications have profoundly influenced the landscape of app design, revolutionizing the way developers create, personalize, and optimize user experiences. These technologies, powered by advanced algorithms and data analytics, enable apps to adapt to user preferences, predict user behavior, and automate complex tasks, ultimately enhancing user engagement and satisfaction. AI and machine learning are integrated into various aspects of app design, from user interface (UI) design and content personalization to performance optimization and security enhancement. By leveraging AI and machine learning, developers can create intelligent apps that learn from user interactions, anticipate user needs, and deliver personalized experiences tailored to individual preferences and behaviors.

One area where AI and machine learning have made significant strides in app design is UI design automation. Traditionally, UI design involves manual creation of layouts, widgets, and navigation structures based on designers' expertise and design principles. However, AI-powered design tools and platforms now offer automated design suggestions, layout recommendations, and color scheme generation based on user input and design preferences. These tools use machine learning algorithms to analyze existing design patterns, user feedback, and industry trends to generate customized UI designs that align with users' preferences and brand aesthetics. For example, Adobe XD, a popular UI/UX design tool, offers a feature called "Auto-Animate" that automatically generates animation effects and transitions based on user interactions, eliminating the need for manual animation creation:

bashCopy code

```
xd      auto-animate      --source=home-screen      --destination=detail-screen
```

This command generates animation effects between the specified source and destination screens in Adobe XD, enhancing the app's user experience.

Another area where AI and machine learning are transforming app design is content personalization. Personalized content recommendations, product suggestions, and user notifications are becoming increasingly common in apps across various industries, from e-commerce and entertainment to social media and news aggregation. Machine learning algorithms analyze user behavior, preferences, and engagement patterns to deliver relevant and timely content tailored to each user's interests and context. For example, recommendation engines use collaborative filtering, content-based filtering, and reinforcement learning techniques to predict user preferences and recommend relevant products or content items. To deploy a recommendation engine in an app, developers can use machine learning frameworks and

libraries such as TensorFlow, PyTorch, or scikit-learn to train recommendation models on historical user data:
bashCopy code

pip install tensorflow

This command installs the TensorFlow library, allowing developers to build and train machine learning models for content recommendation.

Moreover, AI and machine learning are driving advancements in app performance optimization, enabling apps to adapt dynamically to changing user demands and environmental conditions. Machine learning algorithms analyze app usage patterns, system resource utilization, and network conditions to optimize app performance, reduce latency, and minimize battery consumption. For example, machine learning-based performance optimization techniques can adjust app settings, prefetch data, and cache resources based on user behavior and network availability, ensuring smooth and responsive app experiences across different devices and network conditions. To deploy machine learning-based performance optimization in an app, developers can integrate performance monitoring and optimization libraries such as Firebase Performance Monitoring for Android or iOS:
bashCopy code

pod install Firebase/Performance

This command installs the Firebase Performance Monitoring SDK for iOS, allowing developers to monitor app performance and optimize resource usage.

Furthermore, AI and machine learning are playing a crucial role in enhancing app security by detecting and mitigating security threats, vulnerabilities, and fraudulent activities.

Machine learning algorithms analyze app usage patterns, user behavior, and network traffic to identify anomalous activities indicative of security breaches or unauthorized access attempts. Additionally, machine learning-based anomaly detection techniques can detect patterns of fraudulent behavior, such as account takeovers, payment fraud, and identity theft, allowing apps to proactively prevent security incidents and protect user data. To deploy machine learning-based security solutions in an app, developers can integrate anomaly detection algorithms and fraud detection models using machine learning frameworks and libraries such as scikit-learn or TensorFlow:

bashCopy code

```
pip install scikit-learn
```

This command installs the scikit-learn library, allowing developers to build and deploy machine learning models for anomaly detection and fraud detection.

In summary, AI and machine learning applications are reshaping the landscape of app design, enabling developers to create intelligent apps that adapt to user preferences, personalize content, optimize performance, and enhance security. By leveraging AI-powered design tools, recommendation engines, performance optimization techniques, and security solutions, developers can deliver highly engaging, personalized, and secure app experiences that meet the evolving needs of users in today's digital era. With continued advancements in AI and machine learning technologies, the future of app design holds immense potential for innovation and transformation, driving the development of intelligent apps that anticipate and fulfill users' needs seamlessly.

BOOK 2
MASTERING DATA-INTENSIVE APP ARCHITECTURE:
ADVANCED TECHNIQUES AND BEST PRACTICES

ROB BOTWRIGHT

Chapter 1: Advanced Data Modeling Strategies

Multidimensional data modeling is a foundational concept in database design, providing a structured framework for organizing and analyzing data across multiple dimensions. Unlike traditional relational data models, which represent data in two-dimensional tables, multidimensional data models organize data into a multidimensional space, where each axis represents a different aspect or attribute of the data. This multidimensional representation enables users to analyze data from various perspectives, facilitating complex analytical queries and business intelligence applications. Multidimensional data modeling is particularly well-suited for OLAP (Online Analytical Processing) systems, decision support systems, and data warehouses, where users need to perform ad-hoc analysis, drill-down operations, and trend analysis on large volumes of historical data.

At the core of multidimensional data modeling is the concept of a "cube," which serves as the primary data structure for organizing multidimensional data. A cube represents a multidimensional space composed of dimensions, measures, and cells. Dimensions represent the different attributes or characteristics of the data, such as time, geography, product, or customer, while measures represent the quantitative values or metrics being analyzed, such as sales revenue, quantity sold, or profit margin. Cells within the cube store the actual data values, corresponding to specific combinations of dimension members. For example, in a sales cube, each cell may represent the total sales revenue for a particular combination of time period, product category, and geographic region.

To create a multidimensional data model, developers typically use specialized modeling techniques and tools, such as dimensional modeling and OLAP cube design methodologies. Dimensional modeling involves identifying and defining key dimensions and measures that describe the business domain and organizing them into a star schema or snowflake schema. In a star schema, the central fact table contains measures surrounded by dimension tables, each representing a different dimension of the data. In a snowflake schema, dimension tables may be further normalized into sub-dimensions, resulting in a more normalized data structure. To create a star schema in a relational database management system (RDBMS) such as PostgreSQL, developers can use SQL commands to define and create dimension and fact tables:

sqlCopy code

CREATE TABLE dim_time (time_id SERIAL PRIMARY KEY, date DATE, year INTEGER, month INTEGER, day INTEGER); CREATE TABLE dim_product (product_id SERIAL PRIMARY KEY, product_name VARCHAR(255), category VARCHAR(255), subcategory VARCHAR(255)); CREATE TABLE fact_sales (time_id INTEGER REFERENCES dim_time(time_id), product_id INTEGER

REFERENCES dim_product(product_id), sales_amount NUMERIC, quantity_sold INTEGER);

This series of SQL commands creates dimension tables for time and product, along with a fact table for sales data, forming the basis of a star schema data model.

Once the dimensional model is defined, developers can use OLAP cube design tools and platforms to create and populate OLAP cubes based on the dimensional model. OLAP cubes are pre-aggregated data structures that store summarized data across multiple dimensions, allowing for fast and efficient analytical queries. Popular OLAP cube design tools include Microsoft SQL Server Analysis Services (SSAS), Oracle OLAP, and IBM Cognos TM1. These tools provide graphical interfaces for defining cube structures, configuring aggregation rules, and populating cubes with data from underlying data sources. For example, to create an OLAP cube in Microsoft SQL Server Analysis Services, developers can use SQL Server Data Tools (SSDT) to design and deploy a multidimensional project:

bashCopy code

```
ssdt.exe         /create         /type:AnalysisServices
/name:MyCubeProject /model:Multidimensional
```

This command creates a new multidimensional project named "MyCubeProject" using SQL Server Data Tools, allowing developers to design and deploy OLAP cubes within the project.

Once the OLAP cube is created and populated with data, users can query and analyze the data using OLAP query languages such as MDX (Multidimensional Expressions) or SQL for OLAP. MDX is a powerful query language specifically designed for querying multidimensional data, enabling users to perform complex analytical queries, slice-and-dice operations, and drill-down analysis. For example, to retrieve sales revenue by product category and year from an OLAP cube using MDX, users can write the following MDX query:

mdxCopy code

```
SELECT [Measures].[Sales Amount] ON COLUMNS,
[Product].[Category].Members ON ROWS FROM
[SalesCube] WHERE [Time].[Year].[2019]
```

This MDX query retrieves sales revenue by product category for the year 2019 from the OLAP cube named "SalesCube."

In addition to OLAP query languages, users can also visualize multidimensional data using OLAP client tools and dashboards, such as Microsoft Excel with the Power Pivot add-in, Tableau, or IBM Cognos. These tools provide interactive visualization capabilities for exploring and analyzing multidimensional data, including pivot tables, charts, and drill-through reports. By leveraging OLAP cubes and multidimensional data modeling techniques, organizations can gain valuable insights into their business operations, identify trends and patterns, and make informed decisions to drive business growth and success. With the increasing availability of cloud-based OLAP services and analytics platforms, multidimensional data modeling is becoming more accessible to organizations of all sizes, empowering them to harness the power of multidimensional analytics for competitive advantage.

NoSQL data modeling techniques have gained prominence in recent years as organizations seek more flexible and scalable solutions for managing large volumes of diverse data. Unlike traditional relational databases, which adhere to a strict schema and tabular structure, NoSQL databases offer a schema-less approach that accommodates various data types, including structured, semi-structured, and unstructured data. This flexibility makes NoSQL databases well-suited for handling the ever-growing volumes of data generated by modern applications, such as social media platforms, IoT devices, and e-commerce websites. NoSQL databases come in various types, including document-oriented, key-value, columnar, and graph databases, each offering unique data modeling capabilities and performance characteristics.

Document-oriented databases, such as MongoDB and Couchbase, are among the most popular NoSQL databases, particularly for applications with complex and evolving data structures. In document-oriented data modeling, data is stored as JSON-like documents, allowing for nested structures, arrays, and flexible schemas. To create a document-oriented data model in MongoDB, developers can use the MongoDB shell to define collections and insert documents:

bashCopy code

```
mongo
```

This command opens the MongoDB shell, allowing developers to interact with the MongoDB database.

javascriptCopy code

use mydatabase

This command switches to the "mydatabase" database in MongoDB.

javascriptCopy code

```
db.createCollection("users")
```

This command creates a collection named "users" in the MongoDB database.

javascriptCopy code

```
db.users.insertOne({ name: "John Doe", age: 30, email: "john@example.com" })
```

This command inserts a document into the "users" collection, representing a user with name, age, and email fields.

Key-value stores, such as Redis and Amazon DynamoDB, offer a simple yet powerful data model based on key-value pairs. In key-value data modeling, each data item is stored as a key-value pair, where the key is a unique identifier and the value is the associated data. Key-value stores excel in scenarios requiring high throughput and low-latency access to data, such as caching, session management, and real-time analytics. To create a key-value data model in Redis, developers can use the Redis command-line interface (CLI) to set and get key-value pairs:

bashCopy code

```
redis-cli
```

This command opens the Redis command-line interface.

bashCopy code

```
SET mykey "Hello, World!"
```

This command sets the value "Hello, World!" for the key "mykey" in Redis.

bashCopy code

GET mykey

This command retrieves the value associated with the key "mykey" from Redis.

Columnar databases, such as Apache Cassandra and Apache HBase, are optimized for storing and querying large volumes of data with high write and read throughput. In columnar data modeling, data is organized into columns rather than rows, allowing for efficient storage and retrieval of data based on column-level access patterns. Columnar databases are well-suited for use cases requiring fast analytics and real-time data processing, such as time series data analysis, log data management, and sensor data processing. To create a columnar data model in Apache Cassandra, developers can use the CQL (Cassandra Query Language) shell to define keyspaces and tables:

bashCopy code

cqlsh

This command opens the CQL shell for interacting with Apache Cassandra.

sqlCopy code

CREATE KEYSPACE mykeyspace WITH replication = {'class': 'SimpleStrategy', 'replication_factor': 1};

This command creates a keyspace named "mykeyspace" in Apache Cassandra.

sqlCopy code

USE mykeyspace;

This command switches to the "mykeyspace" keyspace in Apache Cassandra.

sqlCopy code

CREATE TABLE users (user_id UUID PRIMARY KEY, name TEXT, email TEXT);

This command creates a table named "users" with columns for user ID, name, and email in Apache Cassandra.

Graph databases, such as Neo4j and Amazon Neptune, are designed for representing and querying graph-like data structures, such as social networks, recommendation engines, and network topologies. In graph data modeling, data is represented as nodes (entities) and edges (relationships) between nodes, enabling rich and expressive data models. Graph databases excel in scenarios requiring complex relationship analysis, pattern matching, and traversal operations. To create a graph data model in Neo4j, developers can use the Neo4j Browser to define nodes, relationships, and properties:

bashCopy code

neo4j-browser

This command opens the Neo4j Browser, allowing developers to interactively define and query graph data.

cypherCopy code

CREATE (john:Person { name: 'John' })

This Cypher query creates a node labeled "Person" with the name property set to 'John' in Neo4j.

cypherCopy code

CREATE (mary:Person { name: 'Mary' })

This Cypher query creates another node labeled "Person" with the name property set to 'Mary' in Neo4j.
cypherCopy code
CREATE (john)-[:FRIENDS_WITH]->(mary)
This Cypher query creates a relationship labeled "FRIENDS_WITH" between the nodes representing John and Mary in Neo4j.

In summary, NoSQL data modeling techniques offer a flexible and scalable approach to managing diverse data types in modern applications. Document-oriented, key-value, columnar, and graph databases each provide unique data modeling capabilities tailored to specific use cases and performance requirements. By understanding the principles and best practices of NoSQL data modeling, developers can design efficient and effective data models that meet the needs of their applications, enabling them to leverage the full potential of NoSQL databases for storing, querying, and analyzing large volumes of data.

Chapter 2: Scalability Patterns and Approaches

Sharding strategies play a pivotal role in distributed database systems, enabling efficient horizontal scaling and improved performance for managing large volumes of data across multiple nodes. Sharding, also known as horizontal partitioning, involves dividing a database into smaller, more manageable subsets called shards, which are distributed across multiple servers or nodes. Each shard contains a distinct subset of the data, allowing for parallel processing of queries and transactions across multiple shards, thereby reducing the overall load on individual nodes and improving scalability. Sharding strategies vary based on factors such as data distribution patterns, workload characteristics, and fault tolerance requirements, and they often involve careful consideration of data partitioning, shard key selection, and data rebalancing techniques to ensure optimal performance and reliability.

One commonly used sharding strategy is range-based sharding, where data is partitioned based on a predefined range of values within a shard key. Range-based sharding is particularly suitable for datasets with natural range queries or temporal data distribution patterns, such as time-series data or geographical data. To implement range-based sharding in a distributed database system like MongoDB, developers can use the MongoDB shell to define shard keys and enable sharding on a collection:

bashCopy code

mongo

This command opens the MongoDB shell for interacting with the MongoDB database.

javascriptCopy code

```
use mydatabase
```

This command switches to the "mydatabase" database in MongoDB.

javascriptCopy code

```
db.createCollection("mycollection", { shardKey: { timestamp: 1 } })
```

This command creates a collection named "mycollection" with a shard key based on the "timestamp" field in MongoDB.

javascriptCopy code

```
sh.shardCollection("mydatabase.mycollection", { timestamp: 1 })
```

This command enables sharding on the "mycollection" collection based on the "timestamp" shard key in MongoDB.

Another sharding strategy is hash-based sharding, where data is partitioned based on the hash value of a shard key. Hash-based sharding evenly distributes data across shards by hashing the shard key values and assigning each hashed value to a specific shard. This approach ensures a more balanced distribution of data and uniform query distribution across shards, making it suitable for datasets with unpredictable access patterns or skewed data distributions. In a distributed database system like Apache Cassandra, developers can enable automatic token-based partitioning to implement hash-based sharding:

bashCopy code

```
cqlsh
```

This command opens the CQL shell for interacting with Apache Cassandra.

sqlCopy code

CREATE KEYSPACE mykeyspace WITH replication = {'class': 'SimpleStrategy', 'replication_factor': 3};

This command creates a keyspace named "mykeyspace" with replication strategy and factor in Apache Cassandra.

sqlCopy code

USE mykeyspace;

This command switches to the "mykeyspace" keyspace in Apache Cassandra.

sqlCopy code

CREATE TABLE mytable (id UUID PRIMARY KEY, data TEXT) WITH CLUSTERING ORDER BY (id ASC);

This command creates a table named "mytable" with a primary key and clustering order in Apache Cassandra.

sqlCopy code

ALTER TABLE mytable WITH compaction = {'class': 'LeveledCompactionStrategy'};

This command configures the compaction strategy for the "mytable" table in Apache Cassandra.

sqlCopy code

ALTER TABLE mytable WITH compression = {'sstable_compression': 'LZ4Compressor'};

This command configures the compression settings for the "mytable" table in Apache Cassandra.

A hybrid sharding strategy combines the benefits of range-based and hash-based sharding to achieve both scalability and data locality. In a hybrid sharding approach, data is initially partitioned based on a range-based strategy to distribute data across shards evenly. Within each shard, further partitioning based on a hash-based strategy is applied to ensure balanced distribution of data and query load. This hybrid approach offers greater flexibility and efficiency in managing both range queries and data distribution, making it suitable for diverse workloads and datasets. To implement a hybrid sharding strategy in a distributed database system like Amazon DynamoDB, developers can use the DynamoDB console or AWS Command Line Interface (CLI) to configure global secondary indexes (GSI) and partition keys:

```
bashCopy code
aws dynamodb create-table --table-name mytable --attribute-definitions
AttributeName=hashkey,AttributeType=S    --key-schema
AttributeName=hashkey,KeyType=HASH       --billing-mode
PAY_PER_REQUEST --region us-west-2
```

This command creates a DynamoDB table named "mytable" with a partition key based on the "hashkey" attribute and sets the billing mode to "PAY_PER_REQUEST" in the US West (Oregon) region.

```
bashCopy code
aws dynamodb update-table --table-name mytable --attribute-definitions
AttributeName=rangekey,AttributeType=N            --global-
secondary-index-updates
'Create={IndexName=myGSI,KeySchema=[{AttributeName
=rangekey,KeyType=HASH}],Projection={ProjectionType=A
LL},ProvisionedThroughput={ReadCapacityUnits=5,WriteC
apacityUnits=5}}' --region us-west-2
```

This command creates a global secondary index named "myGSI" on the "mytable" table with a partition key based on the "rangekey" attribute and provisioned throughput capacity in the US West (Oregon) region.

In addition to these sharding strategies, developers should also consider data rebalancing techniques and shard management practices to ensure the efficient distribution and maintenance of shards over time. Automated shard rebalancing mechanisms and monitoring tools can help detect and mitigate data hotspots, uneven shard distributions, and performance bottlenecks, ensuring the scalability, reliability, and performance of sharded database systems. By understanding and implementing effective sharding strategies and best practices, developers can harness the full potential of distributed database systems to handle massive datasets and support the growing demands of modern applications.

Elastic scaling methods are crucial for modern applications that need to adapt dynamically to varying workloads and resource demands. Unlike traditional scaling approaches that rely on fixed hardware configurations, elastic scaling allows applications to automatically adjust their capacity based on changing demand patterns, ensuring optimal performance, resource utilization, and cost efficiency. Elastic scaling methods encompass a range of techniques and technologies designed to scale application resources, such as compute, storage, and network capacity, up or down dynamically in response to workload fluctuations. These methods enable applications to handle sudden spikes in traffic, accommodate seasonal variations, and efficiently utilize resources during off-peak periods, ultimately enhancing reliability and user experience.

One of the fundamental elastic scaling methods is horizontal scaling, also known as scaling out, which involves adding more instances or nodes to distribute the workload across multiple resources. Horizontal scaling is particularly effective for stateless and parallelizable workloads, such as web servers, microservices, and containerized applications. Cloud computing platforms like Amazon Web Services (AWS), Microsoft Azure, and Google Cloud Platform (GCP) provide built-in support for horizontal scaling through auto-scaling groups or managed services. To enable horizontal scaling in AWS using auto-scaling groups, developers can use the AWS Management Console or AWS Command Line Interface (CLI) to configure scaling policies and thresholds:

```
bashCopy code
aws autoscaling create-auto-scaling-group --auto-scaling-group-name myASG --launch-configuration-name myLaunchConfig --min-size 1 --max-size 10 --desired-capacity 2 --availability-zones us-east-1a us-east-1b --vpc-zone-identifier subnet-12345678 subnet-87654321
```

This command creates an auto-scaling group named "myASG" with a minimum size of 1 instance, a maximum size of 10 instances, and a desired capacity of 2 instances in the specified availability zones and subnets in the US East (N. Virginia) region.

Another elastic scaling method is vertical scaling, also known as scaling up, which involves increasing the capacity of individual resources, such as CPU, memory, or storage, within a single instance or node. Vertical scaling is typically used for applications with monolithic architectures or stateful workloads that cannot be easily distributed across multiple instances. Cloud providers offer various options for vertical scaling, such as instance resizing, managed instance types, and resource allocation policies. In AWS, developers can use the Amazon EC2 console or AWS CLI to resize instances to larger or smaller sizes:

bashCopy code

```
aws ec2 modify-instance-type --instance-id i-1234567890abcdef0 --instance-type t3.large
```

This command modifies the instance type of the specified EC2 instance to "t3.large" using the AWS CLI.

Additionally, auto-scaling policies and triggers can be configured to automate vertical scaling based on predefined thresholds or performance metrics, such as CPU utilization or memory usage.

A hybrid scaling approach combines horizontal and vertical scaling methods to achieve optimal resource utilization and performance. In a hybrid scaling model, applications dynamically scale out by adding more instances to handle increasing workloads, while also vertically scaling individual instances to accommodate higher resource demands within each instance. This approach allows applications to scale both horizontally and vertically as needed, providing greater flexibility and efficiency in resource management. Cloud-native orchestration platforms like Kubernetes and Docker Swarm support hybrid scaling by allowing applications to scale horizontally across multiple nodes and vertically within each node. To deploy a hybrid scaling setup using Kubernetes, developers can define horizontal and vertical scaling policies in the Kubernetes deployment manifests:

yamlCopy code

```yaml
apiVersion: apps/v1 kind: Deployment metadata:
name: my-deployment spec: replicas: 3 selector:
matchLabels: app: my-app template: metadata: labels:
app: my-app spec: containers: - name: my-container
image: my-image resources: requests: cpu: "200m"
memory: "512Mi" limits: cpu: "1" memory: "2Gi"
```

This Kubernetes deployment manifest specifies a
deployment with 3 replicas and defines resource requests
and limits for CPU and memory for each container.

Another important aspect of elastic scaling is auto-scaling
policies and triggers, which allow applications to
automatically scale resources based on predefined
conditions or metrics. Cloud providers offer auto-scaling
features that can be configured to scale resources
dynamically in response to changes in demand or
performance metrics. For example, in AWS, developers
can create CloudWatch alarms to monitor metrics such as
CPU utilization, network traffic, or queue length, and
trigger auto-scaling actions based on predefined
thresholds:

```bash
bashCopy code
aws cloudwatch put-metric-alarm --alarm-name my-cpu-
alarm --alarm-description "Alarm for CPU utilization" --
metric-name CPUUtilization --namespace AWS/EC2 --
statistic Average --period 300 --threshold 70 --
comparison-operator GreaterThanThreshold --dimensions
Name=InstanceId,Value=i-1234567890abcdef0         --
evaluation-periods        2        --alarm-actions
arn:aws:autoscaling:us-east-
1:123456789012:autoScalingGroupName/myASG:policyN
ame/ScaleUp
```

This command creates a CloudWatch alarm named "my-cpu-alarm" to monitor CPU utilization on the specified EC2 instance and triggers the "ScaleUp" auto-scaling policy when the CPU utilization exceeds 70% for two consecutive evaluation periods.

In summary, elastic scaling methods are essential for modern applications to dynamically adjust their capacity and resources in response to changing workloads and demands. Horizontal scaling, vertical scaling, and hybrid scaling approaches provide flexible and efficient ways to scale applications across multiple instances or nodes, optimize resource utilization, and ensure high availability and performance. By leveraging cloud-native scaling features, auto-scaling policies, and orchestration platforms, developers can build scalable and resilient applications that can handle unpredictable traffic patterns and effectively utilize resources in cloud environments.

Chapter 3: Fault Tolerance in Complex Architectures

Chaos engineering practices have emerged as a critical methodology for enhancing the reliability, resilience, and performance of distributed systems and cloud-native applications. Rooted in the philosophy of proactively introducing controlled chaos into systems to uncover weaknesses and vulnerabilities, chaos engineering aims to identify and address potential failure points before they impact end-users. By deliberately injecting faults, failures, and disruptions into production environments, organizations can gain valuable insights into the behavior of their systems under adverse conditions, validate their assumptions about system behavior, and improve their overall fault tolerance and disaster recovery capabilities. Chaos engineering practices encompass a range of techniques, tools, and best practices for designing, implementing, and executing chaos experiments, as well as for analyzing and mitigating the impact of failures.

One of the foundational principles of chaos engineering is the concept of "blast radius," which refers to the scope or extent of the impact that a failure or fault can have on a system. To minimize the blast radius and limit the potential impact of chaos experiments on production environments, organizations often start by conducting experiments in controlled and isolated testing environments, such as staging or pre-production environments. This allows teams to validate the safety and efficacy of their chaos experiments before applying them to production systems. In Kubernetes, for example, developers can use namespaces to create isolated environments for conducting chaos experiments:

bashCopy code

kubectl create namespace chaos-test

This command creates a new namespace named "chaos-test" in Kubernetes, providing an isolated environment for conducting chaos experiments.

Once the testing environment is set up, teams can begin designing and executing chaos experiments by identifying potential failure scenarios, defining hypotheses about system behavior, and selecting appropriate chaos injection techniques. Common chaos injection techniques include introducing latency, disrupting network communication, simulating resource exhaustion, and terminating processes or containers. Tools like Chaos Monkey, developed by Netflix, and Litmus Chaos provide frameworks and libraries for orchestrating chaos experiments and injecting faults into distributed systems. For example, to inject latency into network communication between microservices in a Kubernetes cluster using Litmus Chaos, developers can define a chaos experiment using a ChaosEngine manifest:

yamlCopy code

apiVersion: litmuschaos.io/v1alpha1 kind: ChaosEngine metadata: name: network-latency-chaos namespace: chaos-test spec: appinfo: appns: default applabel: 'app=frontend' chaosServiceAccount: litmus experiments: - name: pod-network-latency spec: components: env: - name: TARGET_CONTAINER value: 'env:TARGET_CONTAINER' definition: kind: PodNetworkChaos ioChaos: true action: delay target:

kind: pod label: 'app=frontend' chaosDuration: '30s' delay: latency: '100ms' correlation: '25%'

This ChaosEngine manifest defines a chaos experiment to inject network latency into pods labeled "app=frontend" in the default namespace for 30 seconds, with a latency of 100 milliseconds and a correlation percentage of 25%.

As chaos experiments are executed and faults are injected into the system, it is essential to monitor and observe the behavior of the system in real-time to identify any unexpected outcomes or negative impacts. Observability tools, monitoring dashboards, and logging systems play a crucial role in providing visibility into system performance, health, and resilience during chaos experiments. Metrics such as latency, error rates, throughput, and system resource utilization can help teams assess the impact of chaos experiments and determine whether the system behaves as expected under stress. Prometheus and Grafana are popular tools for monitoring and visualizing metrics in Kubernetes environments, allowing developers to create custom dashboards to track the performance of their applications and infrastructure:

bashCopy code

```
kubectl apply -f https://raw.githubusercontent.com/kubernetes/ingress-nginx/master/deploy/static/provider/cloud/deploy.yaml
```

This command deploys the NGINX Ingress Controller in a Kubernetes cluster using the provided YAML manifest, enabling external access to services running in the cluster.

bashCopy code

```
kubectl port-forward -n monitoring service/prometheus-server 9090:80
```

This command creates a port forward to access the Prometheus dashboard running in the "monitoring" namespace on port 9090.

bashCopy code

```
kubectl port-forward -n monitoring service/grafana 3000:80
```

This command creates a port forward to access the Grafana dashboard running in the "monitoring" namespace on port 3000.

By analyzing the metrics and telemetry data collected during chaos experiments, teams can gain insights into system behavior, identify potential weaknesses or failure modes, and iteratively improve the resilience and reliability of their applications and infrastructure. Additionally, post-mortem analyses and blameless retrospectives can help teams learn from incidents and failures, identify root causes, and implement preventive measures to mitigate similar issues in the future. Overall, chaos engineering practices provide organizations with a systematic approach to building more robust and resilient systems that can withstand unexpected failures and disruptions in today's complex and dynamic IT environments.

Distributed system resilience techniques are fundamental strategies and practices employed to ensure the robustness, reliability, and fault tolerance of distributed systems in the face of failures, disruptions, and unexpected events. These techniques are essential for maintaining system availability, performance, and data consistency in complex distributed environments where failures are inevitable. Distributed systems consist of interconnected components running on multiple nodes across a network, and ensuring their resilience requires proactive measures to detect, tolerate, and recover from failures gracefully. Resilience techniques encompass a broad range of approaches, including fault tolerance mechanisms, redundancy strategies, failure detection mechanisms, and recovery procedures, all aimed at minimizing the impact of failures and ensuring uninterrupted operation of distributed systems.

One of the primary resilience techniques used in distributed systems is redundancy, which involves duplicating critical components, data, or resources to mitigate the effects of failures. Redundancy can be achieved at various levels of the system stack, including hardware, software, and data layers. At the hardware level, redundant components such as power supplies, network interfaces, and storage devices can be deployed to ensure continuous operation in the event of hardware failures. In cloud computing environments, providers offer redundancy options such as availability zones and regions to distribute resources across geographically separated data centers. For example, in Amazon Web Services (AWS), developers can use the AWS CLI to deploy resources across multiple availability zones:

bashCopy code

```
aws ec2 run-instances --image-id ami-12345678 --count 1
--instance-type t2.micro --key-name MyKeyPair --subnet-
id subnet-12345678 --availability-zone us-east-1a
```

This command launches a new EC2 instance in the specified subnet and availability zone in the US East (N. Virginia) region.

At the software level, redundancy techniques such as replication and failover mechanisms are commonly employed to ensure continuous operation of distributed applications. Replication involves maintaining multiple copies of data or services across multiple nodes to provide fault tolerance and high availability. For instance, databases like Apache Cassandra and MongoDB support data replication across multiple nodes to ensure data durability and availability in the event of node failures. In Apache Cassandra, developers can use the nodetool utility to manage data replication and consistency:

bashCopy code

```
nodetool repair
```

This command performs incremental repairs on data replicas in an Apache Cassandra cluster to ensure consistency and data integrity.

Failover mechanisms enable seamless transition to backup resources or nodes in case of primary resource failures. In Kubernetes, for example, developers can configure pod and service replication controllers to automatically restart failed pods or redirect traffic to healthy pods:

bashCopy code

```
kubectl scale deployment my-deployment --replicas=3
```

This command scales up the number of replicas for the "my-deployment" deployment to 3 in a Kubernetes cluster.

In addition to redundancy, distributed systems employ fault tolerance mechanisms to detect, isolate, and recover from failures without compromising system integrity or performance. Fault tolerance techniques include error detection and handling mechanisms, graceful degradation strategies, and circuit breaker patterns. Error detection mechanisms such as health checks, heartbeat monitoring, and watchdog timers are used to identify and diagnose failures in distributed systems. For example, in microservices architectures, service meshes like Istio and Linkerd provide built-in capabilities for implementing health checks and circuit breaking to detect and handle service failures:

bashCopy code

```
istioctl analyze
```

This command analyzes the Istio configuration and detects potential issues or misconfigurations in a Kubernetes cluster.

Graceful degradation strategies involve dynamically adjusting system behavior or reducing functionality to maintain essential services and prioritize critical operations during failures or degraded conditions. Circuit breaker patterns, inspired by electrical circuit breakers, are used to prevent cascading failures and overload situations by temporarily halting requests to a failing service or component until it recovers:

bashCopy code

```
istioctl create -f circuit-breaker.yaml
```

This command creates a circuit breaker configuration for a service in Istio using a YAML manifest file.

Furthermore, distributed systems leverage automated recovery procedures and self-healing mechanisms to restore system functionality and data integrity after failures. Recovery procedures include rollback mechanisms, state restoration processes, and data consistency checks to recover from failures and inconsistencies introduced during failure events. Automated recovery mechanisms, such as Kubernetes' pod restart policies and stateful set controllers, enable automatic recovery of failed pods and stateful applications:

bashCopy code

```
kubectl delete pod my-pod
```

This command deletes the specified pod from a Kubernetes cluster, triggering the Kubernetes controller to automatically restart the pod based on its restart policy.

Overall, distributed system resilience techniques are essential for ensuring the reliability, availability, and performance of distributed applications in the face of failures and disruptions. By implementing redundancy, fault tolerance mechanisms, and automated recovery procedures, organizations can build resilient distributed systems capable of withstanding failures and delivering uninterrupted services to users.

Chapter 4: Stream Processing and Real-Time Analytics

Event Sourcing and Command Query Responsibility Segregation (CQRS) are two complementary architectural patterns that are increasingly being adopted in the design and implementation of modern distributed systems and microservices-based applications. Event Sourcing is a pattern that emphasizes capturing all changes to an application's state as a sequence of immutable events, rather than storing the current state of the system in a traditional database. In Event Sourcing, each state change or command that affects the application is represented as an event, which is appended to an event log or journal. This log serves as the single source of truth for the application's state history, enabling developers to reconstruct the current state of the system by replaying the events sequentially. Event Sourcing provides several benefits, including auditability, scalability, and resilience, as it allows developers to track the full history of state changes, scale out read-heavy workloads, and recover from failures by replaying events to restore application state.

To implement Event Sourcing in practice, developers typically use event sourcing frameworks or libraries that provide abstractions for defining events, event handlers, and event storage mechanisms. For example, in a Java-based microservices architecture, developers can use the Axon Framework to implement Event Sourcing:
bashCopy code

```
mvn    archetype:generate    -DgroupId=com.example    -
DartifactId=my-project                                 -
DarchetypeGroupId=org.apache.maven.archetypes          -
DarchetypeArtifactId=maven-archetype-quickstart        -
DinteractiveMode=false
```

This Maven command generates a new Maven project with the specified artifact ID and group ID.

Once the project is created, developers can add the Axon Framework dependencies to the project's Maven POM file and define domain events, aggregate roots, and event handlers using Axon's annotations and APIs.

xmlCopy code

```xml
<dependency> <groupId> org.axonframework </groupId>
<artifactId> axon-spring-boot-starter </artifactId>
<version> 4.5.3 </version> </dependency>
```

This XML snippet adds the Axon Framework Spring Boot starter dependency to the project's Maven POM file.

javaCopy code

```java
@Aggregate public class AccountAggregate {
@AggregateIdentifier private String accountId; private
BigDecimal balance; @CommandHandler public
AccountAggregate(CreateAccountCommand command) {
apply( new
AccountCreatedEvent (command.getAccountId(),
command.getInitialBalance())); } @EventSourcingHandler
public void on(AccountCreatedEvent event) {
this.accountId = event.getAccountId(); this.balance =
event.getInitialBalance(); } // Additional command and
event handler methods... }
```

This Java code defines an Axon aggregate root class representing an account entity, along with command and event handler methods for handling account creation commands and events.

In contrast to Event Sourcing, CQRS is an architectural pattern that separates the responsibility for handling read and write operations in a distributed system. In a CQRS architecture, commands that mutate the system's state are handled separately from queries that retrieve data from the system. This separation allows developers to optimize read and write operations independently, as read-heavy workloads can be scaled out separately from write-heavy operations. CQRS often involves maintaining separate data models for reads and writes, with specialized query-side components optimized for querying and presenting data to clients. By decoupling read and write operations, CQRS enables developers to design more scalable, responsive, and maintainable systems, as each side of the system can be optimized for its specific requirements and access patterns.

To implement CQRS in practice, developers can use CQRS frameworks or libraries that provide abstractions for defining commands, queries, command handlers, and query handlers. For example, in a .NET Core microservices architecture, developers can use the MediatR library to implement CQRS:

bashCopy code

dotnet new webapi -n MyProject

This .NET Core CLI command creates a new Web API project named "MyProject" using the default template.

Once the project is created, developers can add the MediatR package to the project's .csproj file and define command and query classes along with their corresponding handlers using MediatR's APIs and conventions.

xmlCopy code

```xml
<ItemGroup> <PackageReference Include="MediatR" Version="11.0.0" /> </ItemGroup>
```

This XML snippet adds the MediatR package reference to the project's .csproj file.

csharpCopy code

```csharp
public class CreateAccountCommand : IRequest<Guid> { public decimal InitialBalance { get; set; } } public class CreateAccountCommandHandler : IRequestHandler<CreateAccountCommand, Guid> { public async Task<Guid> Handle(CreateAccountCommand request, CancellationToken cancellationToken) { // Logic for handling account creation command... return Guid.NewGuid(); } }
```

This C# code defines a command class representing an account creation command and a corresponding command handler class responsible for handling the command and returning the result.

By combining Event Sourcing and CQRS, developers can build scalable, resilient, and maintainable distributed systems that capture the full history of state changes, optimize read and write operations independently, and provide consistent and responsive user experiences. While Event Sourcing ensures data consistency and auditability by capturing all state changes as immutable events, CQRS enables developers to optimize read and write operations separately, improving system scalability and performance. Together, these patterns provide a powerful foundation for building event-driven, microservices-based architectures capable of meeting the demands of modern, data-intensive applications.

Apache Kafka and stream processing frameworks have revolutionized the way modern data-intensive applications handle real-time data ingestion, processing, and analysis. Apache Kafka, an open-source distributed event streaming platform, serves as the backbone for building scalable, fault-tolerant, and highly available streaming data pipelines. Kafka enables applications to publish and subscribe to streams of records, providing a durable and fault-tolerant mechanism for storing and processing real-time data. Kafka's architecture is based on a distributed commit log, where messages are persisted on disk and replicated across multiple brokers for fault tolerance. This architecture allows Kafka to handle high-throughput, low-latency data streams at scale, making it suitable for a wide range of use cases, including log aggregation, event sourcing, stream processing, and real-time analytics.

To deploy Apache Kafka, developers can use Kafka's official Docker images to spin up Kafka clusters locally for development and testing purposes. For example, to start a single-node Kafka cluster using Docker Compose, developers can create a **docker-compose.yml** file with the following configuration:

yamlCopy code

```
version: '3' services: zookeeper: image:
wurstmeister/zookeeper ports: - "2181:2181" kafka:
image: wurstmeister/kafka ports: - "9092:9092"
environment: KAFKA_ADVERTISED_LISTENERS:
INSIDE://kafka:9093,OUTSIDE://localhost:9092
```

```
KAFKA_LISTENER_SECURITY_PROTOCOL_MAP:
INSIDE:PLAINTEXT,OUTSIDE:PLAINTEXT
KAFKA_LISTENERS:
INSIDE://0.0.0.0:9093,OUTSIDE://0.0.0.0:9092
KAFKA_INTER_BROKER_LISTENER_NAME:            INSIDE
KAFKA_ZOOKEEPER_CONNECT:           zookeeper:2181
depends_on: - zookeeper
```

This Docker Compose configuration defines two services: ZooKeeper, which is a required dependency for Kafka, and Kafka itself. The Kafka service is configured to expose ports 9092 for external communication and 9093 for internal communication among Kafka brokers.

Once the Kafka cluster is up and running, developers can interact with it using the Kafka command-line interface (CLI) tool provided by Apache Kafka. For example, to create a new topic named "my-topic" with three partitions and a replication factor of two, developers can use the following command:

```
bashCopy code
kafka-topics.sh --create --topic my-topic --partitions 3 --
replication-factor 2 --bootstrap-server localhost:9092
```

This Kafka CLI command creates a new topic named "my-topic" with three partitions and a replication factor of two, using the Kafka broker running on localhost:9092 as the bootstrap server.

In addition to Kafka's core capabilities for data ingestion and storage, stream processing frameworks built on top of Kafka, such as Apache Flink, Apache Spark Streaming, and Kafka Streams, provide powerful tools for performing real-time data processing and analytics. These frameworks enable developers to build complex data processing pipelines that consume data from Kafka topics, perform transformations and computations on the data streams, and produce results back to Kafka or other downstream systems. Apache Flink, for example, is a stream processing framework that provides support for stateful stream processing, event time processing, and exactly-once semantics, making it suitable for a wide range of streaming use cases, including event-driven applications, IoT analytics, and fraud detection.

To deploy Apache Flink, developers can use Flink's standalone cluster mode or deploy Flink jobs on a managed streaming platform like Apache Flink on Amazon Web Services (AWS) or Google Cloud Platform (GCP). For example, to deploy a Flink job on AWS using the Apache Flink on Amazon EMR service, developers can use the AWS Management Console or AWS CLI to create a new EMR cluster with Flink installed:

bashCopy code

```
aws emr create-cluster --name MyFlinkCluster --release-label emr-6.5.0 --instance-type m5.xlarge --instance-count 2 --applications Name=Flink --ec2-attributes KeyName=my-key-pair --use-default-roles
```

This AWS CLI command creates a new EMR cluster named "MyFlinkCluster" with two m5.xlarge instances and Apache Flink installed, using the specified EC2 key pair for SSH access.

Once the Flink cluster is running, developers can submit Flink jobs to the cluster using the Flink CLI or Flink REST API. For example, to submit a Flink job to count the number of words in a Kafka topic using Flink's DataStream API, developers can write a Java or Scala program and use the Flink CLI to submit the job to the cluster:

bashCopy code

```
flink    run    -c    com.example.WordCountJob
/path/to/wordcount.jar --input-topic my-topic --output-
topic    word-count-results    --bootstrap.servers
localhost:9092
```

This Flink CLI command submits a Flink job to the cluster, specifying the main class (**com.example.WordCountJob**) and input/output topics for the job, as well as the Kafka bootstrap servers.

Overall, Apache Kafka and stream processing frameworks provide a powerful foundation for building scalable, real-time data processing and analytics applications. By leveraging Kafka's distributed event streaming platform and stream processing frameworks like Apache Flink, developers can build robust, scalable, and responsive streaming data pipelines capable of handling large volumes of data with low latency and high throughput. From event-driven architectures to real-time analytics and machine learning applications, Kafka and stream processing frameworks offer a versatile and flexible platform for building next-generation data-intensive applications.

Chapter 5: Distributed Systems Design

Consistency models in distributed systems play a crucial role in defining how data consistency is maintained across multiple nodes in a distributed environment. Consistency refers to the agreement or synchronization of data across different replicas or partitions in a distributed system. Various consistency models exist, each offering different guarantees regarding the visibility of data updates and the order in which they are observed by clients. The choice of consistency model depends on the specific requirements of the application, including factors such as performance, availability, and fault tolerance.

One of the most well-known consistency models is the Strong Consistency model, which guarantees that all read and write operations appear to be instantaneous and linearizable. In a system that enforces strong consistency, clients observe a single, globally ordered sequence of operations, ensuring that all replicas agree on the most recent state of the data. This strong guarantee comes at the cost of increased latency and reduced availability, as the system must coordinate writes across all replicas to maintain consistency.

To implement strong consistency in practice, developers can configure distributed databases like Apache Cassandra or MongoDB to use quorum-based consistency levels for read and write operations. For example, in Apache Cassandra, developers can use the CQL (Cassandra Query Language) shell to configure the consistency level for a read operation:

bashCopy code

```
cqlsh -e "CONSISTENCY QUORUM; SELECT * FROM my_table WHERE id = '123';"
```

This CQL command sets the consistency level to QUORUM for the SELECT query, ensuring that the query returns data from a majority of replicas to ensure consistency.

Another consistency model commonly used in distributed systems is Eventual Consistency, which relaxes the consistency requirements to achieve higher availability and lower latency. In an eventually consistent system, updates are propagated asynchronously to replicas, and there is no guarantee that all replicas will immediately reflect the latest changes. Instead, eventual consistency allows replicas to eventually converge to a consistent state over time, even in the presence of network partitions or failures. While eventual consistency provides better availability and performance compared to strong consistency, it introduces the risk of stale reads and temporary inconsistencies between replicas.

To implement eventual consistency, developers can use distributed databases like Amazon DynamoDB or Riak, which offer tunable consistency levels to balance consistency and availability based on application requirements. For example, in Amazon DynamoDB, developers can specify the desired consistency level when performing read operations using the AWS CLI:

bashCopy code

```
aws dynamodb get-item --table-name my-table --key '{"id": {"S": "123"}}' --consistent-read
```

This AWS CLI command performs a strongly consistent read operation on the "my-table" DynamoDB table, ensuring that the returned data reflects the latest updates.

Additionally, some distributed systems employ a hybrid approach known as Consistent Prefix Consistency, which combines elements of both strong and eventual consistency. In a system with consistent prefix consistency, updates are ordered and applied sequentially across replicas, ensuring that all replicas observe a consistent prefix of the update sequence. While consistent prefix consistency provides stronger guarantees than eventual consistency, it allows for greater flexibility and scalability compared to strong consistency.

To implement consistent prefix consistency, developers can use distributed data stores like Google Cloud Spanner or Apache HBase, which provide linearizable consistency for multi-row transactions. For example, in Google Cloud Spanner, developers can use the gcloud CLI to execute transactions with strong consistency:

bashCopy code

```
gcloud spanner databases execute-sql my-database --sql="SELECT * FROM my_table WHERE id = '123';" --strong
```

This gcloud CLI command executes an SQL query with strong consistency on the "my-database" Google Cloud Spanner database, ensuring that the query reflects the latest updates across all replicas.

Overall, consistency models play a critical role in determining how data is replicated, distributed, and accessed in distributed systems. By understanding the trade-offs between strong consistency, eventual consistency, and other consistency models, developers can design and deploy distributed systems that meet the specific requirements of their applications while balancing factors such as consistency, availability, and performance.

The CAP theorem, also known as Brewer's theorem, is a fundamental principle in the design and operation of distributed systems that highlights the trade-offs between Consistency, Availability, and Partition tolerance. According to the CAP theorem, it is impossible for a distributed system to simultaneously provide all three guarantees—consistency, availability, and partition tolerance—in the event of a network partition. Instead, distributed systems must make trade-offs between these properties, prioritizing one or two at the expense of the third. Consistency refers to the requirement that all nodes in a distributed system have the same view of the data at the same time, ensuring that updates are applied uniformly and atomically across all replicas. Achieving strong consistency ensures that clients always observe the most recent state of the data, but it may come at the cost of increased latency and reduced availability during network partitions or failures.

To deploy a distributed system with strong consistency, developers can use distributed databases like Apache Cassandra or Google Cloud Spanner, which offer tunable consistency levels to balance consistency and availability based on application requirements. For example, in Apache Cassandra, developers can configure the consistency level for read and write operations using the CQL shell:

bashCopy code

```
cqlsh -e "CONSISTENCY QUORUM; SELECT * FROM my_table WHERE id = '123';"
```

This CQL command sets the consistency level to QUORUM for the SELECT query, ensuring that the query returns data from a majority of replicas to ensure consistency.

Availability, on the other hand, refers to the guarantee that every request received by a distributed system will receive a response, even in the presence of network failures or node crashes. Achieving high availability requires distributing data and processing across multiple nodes and ensuring that the system can continue to operate and serve requests even when individual nodes or components fail. However, prioritizing availability may lead to eventual consistency or relaxed consistency guarantees, as the system may sacrifice consistency to maintain responsiveness and uptime.

To deploy a distributed system with high availability, developers can use distributed data stores like Amazon DynamoDB or Apache Cassandra, which are designed to operate reliably in distributed environments with multiple replicas and automatic failover mechanisms. For example, in Amazon DynamoDB, developers can enable automatic scaling and replication for tables to ensure high availability and fault tolerance:

bashCopy code

```
aws dynamodb create-table --table-name my-table --attribute-definitions AttributeName=id,AttributeType=S --key-schema AttributeName=id,KeyType=HASH --billing-mode PAY_PER_REQUEST --stream-specification StreamEnabled=true,StreamViewType=NEW_AND_OLD_IMAGES
```

This AWS CLI command creates a new DynamoDB table named "my-table" with automatic scaling and replication enabled, ensuring high availability and fault tolerance.

Partition tolerance refers to the ability of a distributed system to continue operating and serving requests even when network partitions occur, resulting in the inability of nodes to communicate with each other. Achieving partition tolerance requires designing distributed algorithms and protocols that can detect and recover from network partitions, ensuring that the system remains available and consistent despite temporary communication failures. However, ensuring partition tolerance may require sacrificing either consistency or availability, as the system must tolerate the possibility of data inconsistencies or temporary unavailability during network partitions.

To deploy a distributed system with partition tolerance, developers can use distributed messaging systems like Apache Kafka or RabbitMQ, which provide fault-tolerant message delivery and replication across multiple brokers or nodes. For example, in Apache Kafka, developers can configure topic replication and partitioning to ensure fault tolerance and high availability:

bashCopy code

```
kafka-topics.sh --create --topic my-topic --partitions 3 --replication-factor 2 --bootstrap-server localhost:9092
```

This Kafka CLI command creates a new topic named "my-topic" with three partitions and a replication factor of two, ensuring fault tolerance and high availability by replicating messages across multiple brokers.

In summary, the CAP theorem provides valuable insights into the trade-offs involved in designing and operating distributed systems. By understanding the implications of consistency, availability, and partition tolerance, developers can make informed decisions about the design and deployment of distributed systems, balancing these properties to meet the specific requirements of their applications while ensuring reliability, scalability, and performance in the face of network failures and partitions.

Chapter 6: Containerization and Orchestration for App Deployment

Docker containerization has revolutionized the way applications are developed, deployed, and managed, offering a lightweight and portable solution for packaging software and its dependencies into a standardized unit for deployment. However, to fully leverage the benefits of Docker containerization, it is essential to follow best practices that ensure security, efficiency, scalability, and maintainability throughout the container lifecycle. One of the fundamental best practices in Docker containerization is to use lightweight base images, such as Alpine Linux or Slim variants of popular Linux distributions, to minimize the size of Docker images and reduce the attack surface. Lightweight base images help improve the performance of containerized applications by reducing the amount of disk space and memory required to run containers, as well as minimizing the time it takes to pull and deploy Docker images from container registries.

To create Docker images with lightweight base images, developers can use Dockerfile directives such as FROM to specify the base image and RUN to install necessary dependencies and packages. For example, to create a Docker image based on Alpine Linux, developers can use the following Dockerfile:

DockerfileCopy code

```
FROM alpine:latest RUN apk --no-cache add \ python3 \
&& pip3 install --upgrade pip setuptools
```

This Dockerfile specifies Alpine Linux as the base image and installs Python 3 and pip package manager using the apk package manager. By using Alpine Linux as the base image, developers can create smaller and more efficient Docker images for their applications.

Another best practice in Docker containerization is to minimize the number of layers in Docker images by combining multiple commands into a single RUN instruction and cleaning up unnecessary files and dependencies after each command. This helps reduce the size of Docker images and improve build performance by reducing the number of layers that need to be created and managed. Additionally, minimizing the number of layers makes Docker images easier to understand and maintain, as it reduces the complexity of the image build process and simplifies troubleshooting and debugging.

To combine multiple commands into a single RUN instruction in a Dockerfile, developers can use the && operator to chain commands together. For example, to install multiple packages and dependencies in a single RUN instruction, developers can use the following Dockerfile:

DockerfileCopy code

```
FROM alpine:latest RUN apk --no-cache add \ python3 \ && pip3 install --upgrade pip setuptools \ && rm -rf /var/cache/apk/*
```

This Dockerfile installs Python 3 and pip using a single RUN instruction and then cleans up the package cache using the rm command to reduce the size of the Docker image.

Additionally, it is important to secure Docker containers by following security best practices such as running containers with non-root users, using Docker Content

Trust to verify the integrity of Docker images, and scanning Docker images for vulnerabilities using security tools like Clair or Anchore. Running containers with non-root users helps mitigate the risk of privilege escalation attacks by limiting the capabilities of containerized applications and reducing the impact of security vulnerabilities.

To run Docker containers with non-root users, developers can specify the USER directive in a Dockerfile to set the user and group ID for the container process. For example, to run a containerized application with a non-root user named "appuser", developers can use the following Dockerfile:

DockerfileCopy code

```
FROM alpine:latest RUN adduser -D appuser USER appuser
```

This Dockerfile creates a new non-root user named "appuser" and sets it as the default user for running the containerized application.

Furthermore, using Docker Content Trust (DCT) helps ensure the integrity and authenticity of Docker images by allowing only trusted publishers to push signed images to Docker registries. DCT uses cryptographic signatures to verify the identity of image publishers and ensure that images have not been tampered with or modified by unauthorized parties. Developers can enable Docker Content Trust by setting the DOCKER_CONTENT_TRUST environment variable to "1" or by configuring Docker to use DCT globally in the Docker configuration file. Once enabled, Docker will only pull and run signed images from trusted publishers, reducing the risk of deploying compromised or malicious Docker images.

To enable Docker Content Trust globally, developers can add the following line to the Docker configuration file (usually located at ~/.docker/config.json):

jsonCopy code

```
{ "experimental": "enabled", "disable-legacy-registry": "true", "content-trust": "1" }
```

This configuration enables Docker Content Trust globally and instructs Docker to require signed images for all pull and run operations.

Additionally, developers can use Docker security scanning tools like Clair or Anchore to scan Docker images for known vulnerabilities and security issues. These tools analyze Docker images for vulnerabilities in their software dependencies, operating system packages, and configuration settings, providing actionable insights and recommendations for improving container security. By regularly scanning Docker images for vulnerabilities and applying security patches and updates, developers can reduce the risk of security breaches and protect their containerized applications from exploitation.

To scan Docker images for vulnerabilities using Clair, developers can use the Clair command-line interface (CLI) tool to analyze Docker images and generate security reports. For example, to scan a Docker image named "my-image" using Clair, developers can use the following command:

bashCopy code

```
clairctl analyze my-image
```

This command analyzes the "my-image" Docker image using Clair and generates a security report with information about any vulnerabilities found in the image.

In summary, Docker containerization offers a powerful and flexible platform for developing, deploying, and managing modern applications, but it is essential to follow best practices to ensure security, efficiency, scalability, and maintainability throughout the container lifecycle. By using lightweight base images, minimizing the number of layers in Docker images, securing containers with non-root users and Docker Content Trust, and scanning Docker images for vulnerabilities, developers can create secure, efficient, and reliable Docker containers that meet the requirements of their applications and environments.

Kubernetes orchestration strategies play a pivotal role in managing containerized applications efficiently and effectively, especially in large-scale production environments. Kubernetes, an open-source container orchestration platform, provides a robust set of features for automating deployment, scaling, and management of containerized workloads across clusters of machines. Understanding Kubernetes orchestration strategies is crucial for optimizing resource utilization, ensuring high availability, and achieving seamless scalability of applications. One fundamental aspect of Kubernetes orchestration is pod scheduling, which involves determining the optimal placement of pods (the smallest deployable units in Kubernetes) onto nodes in the cluster based on resource requirements, affinity/anti-affinity rules, and other constraints. Kubernetes uses a scheduling algorithm to assign pods to nodes, taking into account factors such as CPU and memory utilization, node capacity, pod priority, and any node selectors or affinity rules specified in the pod's configuration.

To deploy a Kubernetes pod and specify scheduling constraints, developers can use Kubernetes manifests, which are YAML or JSON files that define the desired state of Kubernetes resources such as pods, deployments, and services. For example, to create a pod with specific resource requests and limits and deploy it to a Kubernetes cluster, developers can create a YAML manifest file like the following:

yamlCopy code
apiVersion: v1 kind: Pod metadata: name: my-pod spec: containers: - name: my-container image: nginx resources: requests: memory: "64Mi" cpu: "250m" limits: memory: "128Mi" cpu: "500m"

This manifest defines a Kubernetes pod named "my-pod" with a single container running the Nginx web server. It specifies resource requests and limits for CPU and memory to ensure that the pod has sufficient resources allocated and to prevent resource contention with other pods running on the same node. Once the manifest is created, developers can deploy the pod to a Kubernetes cluster using the kubectl apply command:

bashCopy code
kubectl apply -f pod.yaml

This command instructs Kubernetes to create or update the pod defined in the YAML manifest file "pod.yaml" and deploy it to the cluster.

Another critical aspect of Kubernetes orchestration is service discovery and load balancing, which involves routing incoming traffic to the appropriate pods in a Kubernetes cluster and distributing the load evenly across multiple instances of a service for optimal performance and scalability. Kubernetes provides built-in support for service discovery and load balancing through the Kubernetes Service abstraction, which acts as a stable endpoint for accessing a set of pods that provide the same functionality. Kubernetes Services use selectors to identify the pods they should route traffic to based on labels assigned to the pods, allowing for dynamic scaling and failover of backend pods without affecting the accessibility of the service.

To deploy a Kubernetes Service and expose it to external traffic, developers can create a Service manifest file similar to the following example:

yamlCopy code

```
apiVersion: v1 kind: Service metadata: name: my-service spec: selector: app: my-app ports: - protocol: TCP port: 80 targetPort: 8080 type: LoadBalancer
```

This manifest defines a Kubernetes Service named "my-service" that routes traffic to pods labeled with the key-value pair "app=my-app." It exposes port 80 on the Service and forwards incoming traffic to port 8080 on the backend pods. Additionally, it specifies the type of Service as "LoadBalancer," which instructs Kubernetes to provision a cloud load balancer (if supported by the underlying cloud provider) to distribute external traffic to the pods.

Once the Service manifest is created, developers can deploy the Service to a Kubernetes cluster using the kubectl apply command:

bashCopy code

```
kubectl apply -f service.yaml
```

This command deploys the Service defined in the YAML manifest file "service.yaml" to the Kubernetes cluster, making it accessible to external clients through the assigned external IP address or domain name.

In addition to pod scheduling and service discovery, Kubernetes orchestration also encompasses other advanced strategies such as horizontal pod autoscaling (HPA), which automatically adjusts the number of replica pods based on resource utilization metrics such as CPU or memory usage. HPA allows Kubernetes to scale applications dynamically in response to changes in workload demand, ensuring optimal performance and resource utilization without manual intervention. To enable horizontal pod autoscaling for a Kubernetes Deployment, developers can use the kubectl autoscale command:

bashCopy code

```
kubectl autoscale deployment my-deployment --cpu-percent=70 --min=2 --max=10
```

This command configures horizontal pod autoscaling for the Kubernetes Deployment named "my-deployment," setting the target CPU utilization to 70% and specifying minimum and maximum numbers of replica pods to maintain.

Overall, Kubernetes orchestration strategies encompass a wide range of techniques and best practices for efficiently managing containerized applications in production environments. By leveraging Kubernetes features such as pod scheduling, service discovery, and horizontal pod autoscaling, developers can build highly resilient, scalable, and maintainable distributed systems that meet the demands of modern cloud-native applications.

Chapter 7: Microservices Architecture: Design and Implementation

Domain-Driven Design (DDD) principles are fundamental guidelines for developing software systems that closely align with the real-world domain they are meant to model, ensuring that the resulting software is more robust, maintainable, and scalable. At the heart of DDD is the concept of domain modeling, which involves capturing and representing the core concepts, behaviors, and relationships of a business domain in software. One of the key principles of DDD is to focus on the domain model as the primary artifact of software development, using techniques such as domain-driven design patterns, domain-specific languages (DSLs), and ubiquitous language to express domain concepts and logic in code effectively. The goal of domain modeling in DDD is to create a shared understanding of the business domain among stakeholders, developers, and users, enabling more effective communication and collaboration throughout the software development process.

To apply DDD principles effectively, developers must first identify and understand the core domain concepts and entities relevant to the problem domain. This involves collaborating closely with domain experts, business analysts, and end-users to elicit domain requirements, analyze business processes, and identify key domain entities, aggregates, and value objects. Once the domain concepts and entities have been identified, developers can use domain-driven design patterns such as Entity,

Value Object, Aggregate, Repository, and Service to model and represent these concepts in code.

For example, consider a banking application that needs to model customer accounts, transactions, and balances. In this scenario, the Account entity could represent a customer account, with attributes such as account number, balance, and account holder information. Additionally, the Transaction entity could represent individual financial transactions, with attributes such as transaction ID, amount, timestamp, and transaction type. By modeling these domain entities using domain-driven design patterns, developers can create a more expressive and maintainable domain model that accurately reflects the underlying business domain.

Another key principle of DDD is to use a ubiquitous language—a shared, consistent vocabulary that is used by all stakeholders to describe domain concepts, processes, and rules. The ubiquitous language helps bridge the communication gap between domain experts and developers, ensuring that everyone involved in the software development process speaks the same language and has a common understanding of domain concepts and requirements. Developers can use domain-specific languages (DSLs) and domain-specific terminology to express domain logic and rules in code, making the codebase more readable, understandable, and maintainable.

To define a ubiquitous language in DDD, developers can work closely with domain experts and stakeholders to identify and document domain terms, concepts, and rules using techniques such as event storming, domain modeling workshops, and domain-driven design tools. By creating a shared vocabulary and language for discussing domain concepts and requirements, developers can ensure that the resulting software accurately reflects the business domain and meets the needs of end-users and stakeholders.

Additionally, DDD emphasizes the importance of bounded contexts—a way to define clear, explicit boundaries around different parts of the domain model to manage complexity and enforce encapsulation. Bounded contexts help break down large, complex domains into smaller, more manageable subdomains, each with its own distinct models, rules, and language. By defining bounded contexts, developers can isolate domain complexity, minimize dependencies between different parts of the system, and improve modularity, scalability, and maintainability.

To implement bounded contexts in DDD, developers can use techniques such as context mapping, subdomain discovery, and context boundaries to identify and define the boundaries of different parts of the domain model. Each bounded context can have its own domain model, ubiquitous language, and set of domain-driven design patterns, tailored to the specific needs and requirements of that subdomain. By defining clear boundaries between bounded contexts, developers can create more cohesive, loosely coupled software systems that are easier to understand, evolve, and maintain.

Furthermore, DDD encourages developers to focus on the core domain—the essential, differentiating aspects of the business domain that provide the most value to the organization. By prioritizing the core domain and allocating resources and effort accordingly, developers can ensure that the resulting software effectively addresses the most critical business needs and delivers maximum business value. DDD advocates for a strategic approach to software development, where developers focus on solving the most challenging and impactful problems within the core domain, while leveraging existing libraries, frameworks, and tools for non-core functionalities.

To identify the core domain in DDD, developers can use techniques such as domain-driven design workshops, domain analysis, and impact mapping to prioritize domain concepts and requirements based on their strategic importance and business value. By focusing on the core domain, developers can build software systems that are more aligned with business goals, more responsive to changing market conditions, and more resilient to technological disruptions.

In summary, Domain-Driven Design (DDD) principles provide valuable guidelines and best practices for developing software systems that closely align with the real-world domain they are meant to model. By focusing on domain modeling, ubiquitous language, bounded contexts, and the core domain, developers can create more robust, maintainable, and scalable software that effectively addresses the needs of end-users and stakeholders. By embracing DDD principles, developers can build software systems that are more resilient to change, more adaptable to evolving business requirements, and more responsive to the dynamic demands of modern business environments.

Service Mesh Implementation for Microservices is a

crucial aspect of modern cloud-native application development, providing a dedicated infrastructure layer for managing communication between microservices. In a microservices architecture, where applications are composed of loosely coupled and independently deployable services, managing service-to-service communication can become complex and challenging. Service mesh addresses this challenge by abstracting away the complexities of network communication and providing features such as service discovery, load balancing, traffic routing, security, and observability. One popular service mesh implementation is Istio, an open-source platform that enables developers to connect, secure, and monitor microservices running on Kubernetes.

To deploy Istio for service mesh implementation, developers can use the istioctl command-line tool, which provides a set of commands for installing, configuring, and managing Istio components on a Kubernetes cluster. The first step is to download the Istio release package from the official Istio website or GitHub repository. Once the Istio package is downloaded, developers can extract it and navigate to the Istio directory:

bashCopy code

```
tar -zxvf istio-1.13.0.tar.gz cd istio-1.13.0
```

Next, developers can install Istio on their Kubernetes cluster using the istioctl command with the install option. By default, Istio is installed in the istio-system namespace:

bashCopy code

```
istioctl install
```

This command installs the core Istio components, including the Istio control plane components (such as Pilot, Citadel, and Galley) and the Envoy proxy sidecar containers, which are injected into each pod to intercept and manage inbound and outbound traffic. Once Istio is installed, developers can deploy their microservices to the Kubernetes cluster and leverage Istio's features for managing service-to-service communication.

One of the key features of Istio is traffic management, which allows developers to control and manipulate the flow of traffic between microservices. Istio provides sophisticated traffic routing capabilities, including support for A/B testing, canary deployments, and blue-green deployments. Developers can use Istio's VirtualService and DestinationRule resources to define traffic routing rules and policies for their microservices.

For example, to configure a blue-green deployment with Istio, developers can define two Kubernetes Services and VirtualServices—one for the blue version of the microservice and one for the green version—and use Istio's traffic routing capabilities to gradually shift traffic from the blue version to the green version:

yamlCopy code

apiVersion: networking.istio.io/v1alpha3 kind: VirtualService metadata: name: my-service spec: hosts: - my-service http: - route: - destination: host: my-service-blue weight: 90 - destination: host: my-service-green weight: 10

This VirtualService configuration specifies that 90% of incoming traffic should be routed to the blue version of the microservice (my-service-blue), while 10% of traffic should be routed to the green version (my-service-green). Developers can gradually adjust the weights to shift more traffic to the green version as it undergoes testing and validation.

In addition to traffic management, Istio provides robust security features for securing communication between microservices. Istio supports mutual TLS (mTLS) encryption, which encrypts traffic between Envoy proxies using certificates, ensuring that communication between microservices is encrypted and authenticated. Istio also provides fine-grained access control policies that allow developers to define who can access which microservices and what operations they can perform.

To enable mTLS encryption in Istio, developers can configure Istio's mesh-wide mutual TLS policy using the istioctl command:

bashCopy code

```
istioctl install --set values.global.mtls.enabled=true
```

This command configures Istio to enforce mutual TLS encryption for all communication between microservices in the mesh. Developers can also define more granular access control policies using Istio's AuthorizationPolicy resource to specify which microservices are allowed to communicate with each other and under what conditions.

Another critical aspect of service mesh implementation with Istio is observability, which enables developers to monitor and troubleshoot microservices and their interactions in real-time. Istio provides built-in support for distributed tracing, metrics collection, and logging, allowing developers to gain insights into the performance, availability, and reliability of their microservices.

To enable observability features in Istio, developers can deploy Istio's monitoring components, such as Prometheus for metrics collection and Grafana for visualization, using the istioctl command:

bashCopy code

```
istioctl install --set profile=demo
```

This command installs Istio with the demo profile, which includes the Prometheus and Grafana add-ons for monitoring. Once installed, developers can access the Grafana dashboard to view metrics such as request latency, error rates, and throughput for their microservices.

Overall, service mesh implementation with Istio provides a powerful platform for managing service-to-service communication in microservices architectures. By leveraging Istio's features for traffic management, security, and observability, developers can build more resilient, scalable, and maintainable microservices applications that meet the demands of modern cloud-native environments.

Chapter 8: Performance Tuning in High-Volume Environments

Profiling and benchmarking techniques are essential tools for developers seeking to optimize the performance of their software applications. Profiling involves analyzing the runtime behavior of an application to identify performance bottlenecks, memory leaks, and CPU usage inefficiencies, while benchmarking involves measuring the performance and scalability of an application under specific conditions. These techniques are critical for ensuring that software applications meet performance requirements, deliver optimal user experiences, and operate efficiently in production environments.

One widely used profiling technique is CPU profiling, which involves measuring the amount of CPU time consumed by different parts of an application during execution. CPU profiling helps developers identify which functions or methods are consuming the most CPU resources and optimize them to reduce execution time and improve overall application performance. One common tool for CPU profiling in the Go programming language is the **pprof** tool, which can be integrated into Go applications to generate CPU profiles and visualize them using tools like **go tool pprof** or **pprof** web interface.

To generate a CPU profile using **pprof**, developers can add import the **net/http/pprof** package into their Go application and expose a HTTP endpoint for collecting CPU profiles:

goCopy code

```
import _ "net/http/pprof"
```

bashCopy code

```
go run main.go
```

Once the application is running, developers can use the **go tool pprof** command to capture a CPU profile:

bashCopy code

```
go              tool              pprof
http://localhost:6060/debug/pprof/profile
```

This command fetches a CPU profile from the application's HTTP endpoint and opens an interactive shell for analyzing the profile data. Developers can use commands like **top**, **list**, and **web** to inspect the profile data and identify hotspots in the code that are consuming excessive CPU time.

Another common profiling technique is memory profiling, which involves analyzing the memory usage of an application to identify memory leaks, inefficient memory allocation patterns, and excessive memory consumption. Memory profiling is especially important for long-running server applications and services to ensure that they remain stable and performant over time. In Go, developers can use the built-in memory profiling capabilities provided by the **runtime/pprof** package to capture memory profiles and analyze them using tools like **go tool pprof** or **pprof** web interface.

To generate a memory profile using **runtime/pprof**, developers can import the package into their Go application and start a memory profiler:

goCopy code

```
import ( "os" "runtime/pprof" ) func main() { f, err :=
os.Create("memprofile") if err != nil { log.Fatal(err) }
defer f.Close() pprof.WriteHeapProfile(f) }
```

This code snippet creates a memory profile file named "memprofile" and writes the memory profile data to it. Developers can then use the **go tool pprof** command to analyze the memory profile:

bashCopy code

```
go tool pprof memprofile
```

This command opens an interactive shell for analyzing the memory profile data and provides commands for inspecting memory allocations, heap usage, and memory growth over time.

In addition to profiling, benchmarking is another important technique for evaluating the performance and scalability of software applications. Benchmarking involves running a series of controlled tests to measure the execution time and resource utilization of an application under different workloads and conditions. In Go, developers can write benchmark functions using the built-in **testing** package and use the **go test** command to run benchmarks and generate performance reports.

goCopy code

```
func BenchmarkMyFunction(b *testing.B) { for i := 0; i
< b.N; i++ { // Run the code being benchmarked result
:= MyFunction() _ = result } }
```

```bash
bashCopy code
go test -bench=.
```

This command runs all benchmark functions in the current package and generates a report showing the execution time and memory allocations for each benchmark. Developers can use the benchmark report to compare the performance of different implementations, identify performance bottlenecks, and optimize critical code paths for better performance. Overall, profiling and benchmarking techniques are essential for optimizing the performance of software applications and ensuring that they meet performance requirements in production environments. By using tools like CPU profiling, memory profiling, and benchmarking, developers can identify performance bottlenecks, optimize critical code paths, and deliver faster, more efficient software applications that provide optimal user experiences and meet the demands of modern cloud-native environments.

Scalable caching strategies play a crucial role in modern software development, especially in distributed systems and microservices architectures, where the need for efficient data retrieval and processing is paramount. Caching involves storing frequently accessed data in a fast-access storage layer, such as memory or a distributed cache, to reduce the latency and load on backend systems. While caching can significantly improve the performance and scalability of applications, designing scalable caching strategies requires careful consideration of factors such as cache invalidation, consistency, and cache eviction policies. One common approach to implementing scalable caching strategies is to use distributed caching solutions such as Redis or Memcached, which provide high-performance, scalable, and fault-tolerant caching services.

To deploy a distributed caching solution like Redis, developers can use container orchestration platforms like Kubernetes to manage and scale the Redis cluster. Kubernetes provides built-in support for deploying stateful applications such as Redis using StatefulSets, which ensure that each Redis instance has a stable, unique identity and persistent storage. To deploy Redis on Kubernetes, developers can create a Redis StatefulSet manifest file specifying the desired configuration and resource requirements:

```
yamlCopy code
apiVersion: apps/v1 kind: StatefulSet metadata:
name: redis spec: serviceName: redis replicas: 3
selector: matchLabels: app: redis template:
metadata: labels: app: redis spec: containers: -
name: redis image: redis:latest ports: -
containerPort: 6379 resources: requests: memory:
"64Mi" cpu: "100m"
```

This manifest file defines a Redis StatefulSet with three replicas, each running the official Redis Docker image and exposing port 6379 for client connections. The StatefulSet ensures that each Redis instance has its own stable network identity and persistent storage volume.

Once the Redis StatefulSet is deployed, developers can use the **kubectl** command-line tool to manage and monitor the Redis cluster. For example, developers can use the **kubectl get pods** command to view the status of Redis pods:

bashCopy code

```
kubectl get pods
```

This command lists all pods in the current Kubernetes namespace, including the Redis pods, along with their status, IP addresses, and other metadata. Developers can use similar **kubectl** commands to inspect the status of other Kubernetes resources, such as services, StatefulSets, and persistent volumes.

In addition to deploying Redis on Kubernetes, developers can also use caching libraries and frameworks to integrate caching into their applications and manage cache interactions programmatically. One popular caching library for Java applications is Spring Cache, which provides a simple and powerful caching abstraction layer that supports various caching providers, including Redis and Ehcache. To integrate Spring Cache with Redis, developers can add the necessary dependencies to their Spring Boot application and configure the cache manager to use Redis as the caching provider:

xmlCopy code

```
<dependency>
<groupId>org.springframework.boot</groupId>
<artifactId>spring-boot-starter-data-redis</artifactId>
</dependency>
```

javaCopy code

```
@Configuration @EnableCaching public class CacheConfig extends CachingConfigurerSupport {
```

```java
@Bean public RedisCacheManager
cacheManager(RedisConnectionFactory
redisConnectionFactory) { return
RedisCacheManager.builder(redisConnectionFactory)
.cacheDefaults(CacheConfiguration.defaultCacheConfig
()) .build(); } }
```

This configuration sets up a Redis cache manager using the Spring Data Redis library, allowing developers to annotate methods in their application with **@Cacheable**, **@CachePut**, and **@CacheEvict** annotations to enable caching and control cache behavior. For example, developers can use the **@Cacheable** annotation to cache the results of expensive method calls:

javaCopy code

```java
@Service public class MyService {
@Cacheable("myCache") public String getData(String
key) { // Expensive computation or database query
return "Data for key " + key; } }
```

This method retrieves data from the cache if it exists, or computes the result and caches it for future invocations if not.

Furthermore, to ensure scalability and fault tolerance in distributed caching environments, developers should consider strategies for cache partitioning, replication, and data sharding. Partitioning involves dividing the cache data into multiple partitions or shards, each managed by a separate cache instance or cluster. Replication involves replicating cache data across multiple cache nodes to ensure high availability and

146

fault tolerance. Data sharding involves distributing cache data evenly across multiple cache nodes based on a sharding key or algorithm, allowing for efficient data retrieval and load balancing.

In summary, scalable caching strategies are essential for improving the performance and scalability of modern software applications, especially in distributed systems and microservices architectures. By leveraging distributed caching solutions like Redis and Memcached, developers can reduce latency, improve throughput, and handle high volumes of concurrent requests more effectively. Additionally, by integrating caching libraries and frameworks like Spring Cache into their applications, developers can manage cache interactions programmatically and control cache behavior with ease. However, designing scalable caching strategies requires careful consideration of factors such as cache invalidation, consistency, and data partitioning to ensure optimal performance and reliability in production environments.

Chapter 9: Advanced Security Protocols and Practices

Zero Trust Security Model is a paradigm shift in cybersecurity that challenges the traditional perimeter-based security approach by assuming that threats could originate from both internal and external sources. In a Zero Trust model, no entity, whether inside or outside the organization's network, is inherently trusted. Instead, each user, device, or application attempting to access resources must undergo strict authentication and authorization processes before being granted access. This approach aims to mitigate the risk of data breaches and unauthorized access by enforcing strict access controls and continuously monitoring and verifying the trustworthiness of users and devices.

Implementing a Zero Trust Security Model requires organizations to adopt a holistic approach to security that encompasses network security, identity and access management (IAM), endpoint security, and data protection. One of the fundamental principles of Zero Trust is the concept of least privilege, which dictates that users should only be granted the minimum level of access necessary to perform their jobs. This principle helps reduce the attack surface and limit the potential impact of security breaches.

To deploy a Zero Trust Security Model, organizations can leverage a combination of technologies and best practices to create a layered security architecture that protects against both internal and external threats. One key technology in Zero Trust architecture is identity and access management (IAM) solutions, which provide centralized control over user authentication and authorization. IAM platforms such as Okta, Azure Active Directory, or AWS IAM allow organizations to define and enforce access policies based on user roles, group memberships, and other attributes.

CLI commands can be used to configure and manage IAM policies and access controls. For example, in AWS IAM, administrators can use the AWS Command Line Interface (CLI) to create IAM policies that define permissions for specific resources:

bashCopy code

```
aws iam create-policy --policy-name MyPolicy --policy-document file://my-policy.json
```

This command creates a new IAM policy named "MyPolicy" using a JSON file ("my-policy.json") that specifies the permissions granted to users or roles.

Another key component of a Zero Trust Security Model is network segmentation, which involves dividing the network into smaller, isolated segments to contain and limit the spread of cyber threats. Network segmentation can be implemented using virtual LANs (VLANs), firewalls, and software-defined networking (SDN) technologies. For example, organizations can use SDN solutions like VMware NSX or Cisco ACI to create micro-segmentation policies that restrict communication between different segments of the network based on predefined rules.

To configure network segmentation using SDN technologies, administrators can use CLI commands provided by the SDN vendor. For instance, in VMware NSX, administrators can use the NSX Command Line Interface (CLI) to create security policies that define traffic flow rules between different segments:

bashCopy code

```
nsxcli network segment create --name FinanceSegment --subnet 192.168.1.0/24 nsxcli security policy create --name FinancePolicy --source FinanceSegment --destination HRSegment --allow tcp/443
```

These commands create a new network segment named "FinanceSegment" with the subnet 192.168.1.0/24 and create a security policy named "FinancePolicy" that allows TCP traffic on port 443 from the FinanceSegment to the HRSegment.

In addition to IAM and network segmentation, encryption plays a vital role in Zero Trust security by protecting data both at rest and in transit. Organizations can use encryption technologies such as Transport Layer Security (TLS) for securing communication channels and encrypting sensitive data stored in databases or filesystems. For example, administrators can enable TLS encryption for web servers using OpenSSL by generating a private key and obtaining a signed certificate from a trusted Certificate Authority (CA):

bashCopy code

```
openssl req -newkey rsa:2048 -nodes -keyout server.key -x509 -days 365 -out server.crt
```

This command generates a new RSA private key and self-signed certificate valid for 365 days, which can be used to secure HTTPS connections.

Furthermore, continuous monitoring and real-time threat detection are essential components of a Zero Trust Security Model, allowing organizations to identify and respond to security incidents promptly. Security Information and Event Management (SIEM) solutions such as Splunk or Elastic Security can help organizations collect, analyze, and correlate security events from various sources to detect and mitigate potential threats. CLI commands can be used to configure and manage SIEM solutions and set up alerts for suspicious activities:

```bash
splunk add monitor /var/log/auth.log -index main
```

This command configures Splunk to monitor the /var/log/auth.log file and index the collected log data in the "main" index for further analysis.

In summary, a Zero Trust Security Model represents a proactive approach to cybersecurity that prioritizes continuous verification, strict access controls, and defense-in-depth strategies to protect against evolving cyber threats. By implementing a Zero Trust architecture and leveraging technologies such as IAM, network segmentation, encryption, and continuous monitoring, organizations can enhance their security posture and mitigate the risks associated with insider threats, external attackers, and advanced persistent threats (APTs).

Secure Multi-Party Computation (SMPC) techniques represent a groundbreaking advancement in the field of cryptography, enabling multiple parties to jointly compute a function over their private inputs while keeping those inputs confidential. These techniques have gained significant attention and adoption in various domains, including finance, healthcare, and privacy-preserving data analytics, where parties need to collaborate and derive insights from sensitive data without revealing it to each other. SMPC protocols provide a mathematical framework for secure collaboration among multiple parties, ensuring privacy, confidentiality, and integrity throughout the computation process.

To deploy SMPC techniques, parties typically follow a set of cryptographic protocols and algorithms designed to achieve secure computation. One such protocol is the Secure Multi-Party Computation Protocol (SMPC), which enables parties to jointly compute a function without revealing their inputs. One widely used algorithm for SMPC is the Yao's Garbled Circuits protocol, which allows parties to compute a circuit-based function securely. The protocol involves the construction of garbled circuits, where each party garbles their input and shares the garbled circuit with other parties. The parties then evaluate the garbled circuit to obtain the result without learning each other's inputs.

To implement Yao's Garbled Circuits protocol, parties can use cryptographic libraries such as Secure Multi-Party Computation Framework (SMPCF), which provides APIs for constructing garbled circuits and evaluating them securely. For example, in a Python environment, parties can use the PySyft library, which implements SMPC protocols and provides high-level abstractions for secure computation tasks:

pythonCopy code

```
from syft.frameworks.torch.circuit import GCircuit from syft.frameworks.torch.smpc import MPCRepo import torch # Define the circuit def add(x, y): return x + y circuit = GCircuit("Addition Circuit", [add]) # Garble the circuit garbled_circuit = circuit.garble() # Share the garbled circuit MPCRepo.shared(garbled_circuit)
```

This code snippet demonstrates how to create a garbled circuit for addition using PySyft and share it among multiple parties using an MPC repository.

Another important aspect of SMPC techniques is secure key generation and management. Parties involved in SMPC protocols typically generate cryptographic keys for encryption, decryption, and authentication purposes, ensuring that only authorized parties can participate in the computation process. Key management solutions such as Key Management Service (KMS) provide APIs for generating, storing, and distributing cryptographic keys securely. For example, in a cloud environment, parties can use cloud service providers' KMS offerings, such as AWS Key Management Service (KMS) or Google Cloud Key Management Service (KMS), to manage cryptographic keys:

bashCopy code

```
# Create a new cryptographic key aws kms create-key --description "SMPC Encryption Key" # Enable key rotation aws kms enable-key-rotation --key-id <key-id>
```

These CLI commands demonstrate how to create a new cryptographic key using AWS KMS and enable key rotation to periodically rotate the encryption key for improved security.

Furthermore, to ensure the integrity and authenticity of data exchanged during SMPC protocols, parties can use cryptographic hash functions and digital signatures to sign and verify messages. Hash functions such as SHA-256 generate fixed-length hashes from variable-length inputs, providing a secure way to verify data integrity. Digital signatures, on the other hand, use public-key cryptography to sign messages, allowing parties to verify the authenticity of the sender. Tools like OpenSSL provide CLI commands for generating hash values and digital signatures:

bashCopy code

```
# Generate SHA-256 hash of a file openssl sha256 <file> # Generate digital signature using private key openssl dgst -sha256 -sign <private-key.pem> -out <signature> <data>
```

These commands illustrate how to generate a SHA-256 hash of a file and create a digital signature using OpenSSL CLI commands.

In addition to cryptographic techniques, secure communication protocols such as Transport Layer Security (TLS) play a crucial role in ensuring the confidentiality and integrity of data exchanged during SMPC protocols. TLS provides end-to-end encryption and authentication mechanisms, protecting data transmitted over insecure networks. Organizations can use TLS libraries such as OpenSSL or libraries provided by programming languages like Python or Java to implement secure communication channels:

pythonCopy code

```
import socket import ssl # Create a TLS connection context = ssl.create_default_context() with socket.create_connection(("example.com", 443)) as sock: with context.wrap_socket(sock, server_hostname="example.com") as ssock: ssock.sendall(b"GET / HTTP/1.1\r\nHost: example.com\r\n\r\n") response = ssock.recv(4096)
```

This Python code snippet demonstrates how to establish a TLS connection with a remote server using the **ssl** module and send an encrypted HTTP request.

In summary, Secure Multi-Party Computation techniques represent a powerful tool for enabling secure collaboration among multiple parties while preserving the privacy and confidentiality of their inputs. By leveraging cryptographic protocols, key management solutions, secure communication protocols, and cryptographic libraries, organizations can deploy SMPC techniques to perform complex computations on sensitive data securely and derive valuable insights without compromising data privacy.

Chapter 10: Governance and Compliance in Data-Intensive Appli

GDPR Compliance Strategies have become paramount for organizations handling personal data, especially since the European Union's General Data Protection Regulation (GDPR) came into effect in 2018. This regulation has significantly impacted how businesses worldwide manage and protect personal data, imposing strict requirements and hefty fines for non-compliance. To ensure adherence to GDPR regulations, organizations must implement robust compliance strategies that encompass various aspects of data protection, privacy management, and regulatory compliance. One fundamental aspect of GDPR compliance is understanding the scope and applicability of the regulation to the organization's operations and data processing activities. This involves conducting a thorough assessment of the types of personal data collected, processed, and stored, as well as identifying the legal basis for data processing activities.

CLI commands can be used to facilitate the data discovery and classification process, helping organizations identify and categorize personal data within their systems. For example, organizations can use data discovery tools such as Apache Ranger or IBM Guardium to scan their data repositories and identify sensitive data:

bashCopy code

ranger-admin start

This command starts the Apache Ranger Admin service, allowing organizations to configure and manage data access policies and conduct data discovery scans.

Once organizations have identified the personal data they process, they must establish data governance frameworks and implement data protection measures to ensure compliance with GDPR requirements. This includes implementing data minimization and purpose limitation principles, which dictate that organizations should only collect and process personal data for specified, explicit, and legitimate purposes. Additionally, organizations must ensure that personal data is accurate, up-to-date, and securely stored, with appropriate security measures in place to prevent unauthorized access or disclosure.

To deploy data protection measures, organizations can use encryption, tokenization, and pseudonymization techniques to safeguard personal data from unauthorized access. For example, organizations can encrypt sensitive data using encryption algorithms such as AES (Advanced Encryption Standard) or RSA (Rivest–Shamir–Adleman):

bashCopy code

```
openssl enc -aes-256-cbc -in data.txt -out data.enc
```

This command encrypts the file "data.txt" using AES-256-CBC encryption and stores the encrypted data in a file named "data.enc".

In addition to data protection measures, organizations must establish procedures for managing data subject rights, such as the right to access, rectification, erasure, and portability of personal data. This involves implementing mechanisms for handling data subject requests, verifying the identity of data subjects, and responding to requests within the mandated timeframe. Organizations can use ticketing systems or customer relationship management (CRM) platforms to manage data subject requests efficiently:

bashCopy code

```
aws sqs create-queue --queue-name data-subject-requests
```

This command creates a new queue named "data-subject-requests" in Amazon Simple Queue Service (SQS), allowing organizations to receive and process data subject requests in a systematic manner.

Furthermore, organizations must ensure that their data processing activities are conducted in accordance with the principles of data protection by design and by default. This involves integrating data protection measures into the design and development of products, services, and systems from the outset. For example, organizations can use Privacy Impact Assessments (PIAs) or Data Protection Impact Assessments (DPIAs) to assess the potential privacy risks associated with new projects or initiatives:

bashCopy code

```
gdpr-cli create-pia --project-name "New Product Launch"
```

This command creates a new Privacy Impact Assessment (PIA) for the project "New Product Launch," allowing organizations to evaluate and mitigate privacy risks associated with the project.

Additionally, organizations must establish processes for monitoring and auditing their GDPR compliance efforts, ensuring ongoing adherence to regulatory requirements. This involves conducting regular compliance audits, assessing the effectiveness of data protection measures, and addressing any identified gaps or deficiencies. Organizations can use compliance management platforms or governance, risk, and compliance (GRC) solutions to streamline compliance monitoring and reporting:

bashCopy code

```
auditctl -a always,exit -F arch=b64 -S open -k file-access
```

This command configures the Linux Audit framework to monitor all file access events and generate audit logs for compliance auditing purposes.

In summary, GDPR compliance strategies require organizations to adopt a comprehensive approach to data protection, privacy management, and regulatory compliance. By implementing robust data governance frameworks, data protection measures, procedures for managing data subject rights, and mechanisms for monitoring compliance, organizations can ensure adherence to GDPR requirements and mitigate the risk of regulatory fines and penalties.

Data Governance Frameworks play a pivotal role in organizations' efforts to manage and protect their data assets effectively. These frameworks encompass a set of policies, processes, and controls designed to ensure the availability, integrity, confidentiality, and usability of data across the enterprise. In today's data-driven landscape, where organizations accumulate vast amounts of data from various sources, establishing a robust data governance framework is essential for maintaining data quality, mitigating risks, and achieving regulatory compliance. One fundamental aspect of data governance frameworks is defining the roles and responsibilities of stakeholders involved in data management and decision-making processes.

To deploy a data governance framework, organizations can use CLI commands to establish data governance committees and assign roles to stakeholders. For example, organizations can use the AWS CLI to create IAM roles for data stewards, data owners, and data custodians:

bashCopy code

```
aws iam create-role --role-name DataStewardRole --assume-role-policy-document file://trust-policy.json
```

This command creates an IAM role named "DataStewardRole" with a trust policy that allows trusted entities to assume the role, enabling data stewards to manage data governance activities within the organization.

Furthermore, data governance frameworks require organizations to define data governance policies and standards that govern how data is managed, accessed, and used across the enterprise. These policies typically cover data classification, data retention, data access controls, data quality, and data privacy, among other aspects. Organizations can use CLI commands to create and enforce data governance policies using tools such as Apache Ranger or AWS Identity and Access Management (IAM):

```bash
bashCopy code
ranger-admin create-policy --service hdfs --policy-name DataClassificationPolicy --policy-file data_classification_policy.json
```

This command creates a data classification policy named "DataClassificationPolicy" for the Hadoop Distributed File System (HDFS) using Apache Ranger, allowing organizations to classify and manage data based on its sensitivity and importance.

In addition to policies, organizations must establish processes for data governance activities, including data discovery, data lineage tracking, data access requests, and data stewardship. Data discovery tools such as Apache Atlas or Collibra can be deployed to identify and catalog data assets across the enterprise:

```bash
bashCopy code
atlascli discover --source database --output data_catalog.json
```

This command initiates a data discovery process using Apache Atlas, scanning databases for data assets and generating a data catalog in JSON format.

Moreover, organizations must implement data quality management processes to ensure that data meets predefined quality standards and is fit for its intended use. Data quality tools such as Talend or Informatica can be deployed to perform data profiling, cleansing, and monitoring activities:

```bash
bashCopy code
```

```
talendcli    profile    --source    database    --output
data_profile.json
```
This command profiles data stored in a database using Talend, identifying data quality issues such as missing values, duplicates, and inconsistencies.

Furthermore, data governance frameworks should include mechanisms for data access control and data security, ensuring that only authorized users can access and manipulate data assets. Access control policies can be enforced using tools such as Apache Sentry or AWS IAM:

bashCopy code

```
sentry-cli  grant  --role  analyst  --privilege  select  --
database sales
```

This command grants the "analyst" role select privilege on the "sales" database using Apache Sentry, allowing analysts to query sales data.

Additionally, organizations must establish processes for data stewardship, where designated individuals are responsible for managing and overseeing data assets within their domains. Data stewardship tools such as Collibra or Alation can be deployed to facilitate data stewardship activities:

bashCopy code

```
alationcli assign-steward --dataset customer --steward
alice@example.com
```

This command assigns Alice as the data steward for the "customer" dataset using Alation, empowering her to manage and govern customer data effectively.

Moreover, data governance frameworks should incorporate mechanisms for monitoring and auditing data governance activities, ensuring ongoing compliance with policies and standards. Monitoring tools such as IBM InfoSphere Information Analyzer or AWS CloudTrail can be deployed to track data access, changes, and usage:

bashCopy code

```
cloudtrail start-logging --name data-governance-logging
```

This command starts logging data governance activities using AWS CloudTrail, capturing API calls and events related to data governance operations.

In summary, data governance frameworks are essential for organizations to manage and protect their data assets effectively. By defining roles and responsibilities, establishing policies and standards, implementing processes and controls, and deploying tools and technologies, organizations can ensure the availability, integrity, confidentiality, and usability of their data assets across the enterprise.

BOOK 3
SCALING APPLICATIONS
STRATEGIES AND TACTICS FOR HANDLING DATA-INTENSIVE WORKLOADS

ROB BOTWRIGHT

Chapter 1: Understanding Scalability in Application Design

Scalability Metrics and Measurement are fundamental aspects of evaluating the performance and effectiveness of systems in handling increasing workloads and growing demands. In today's dynamic and fast-paced digital landscape, where businesses constantly strive to accommodate larger user bases, higher data volumes, and more complex processing tasks, understanding scalability metrics is crucial for ensuring that systems can scale efficiently to meet evolving needs. Scalability metrics encompass a range of key performance indicators (KPIs) and benchmarks that assess various aspects of a system's scalability, including its ability to handle increased traffic, process larger datasets, and accommodate growing numbers of users or transactions.

To effectively measure scalability, organizations need to define relevant metrics that align with their specific objectives and requirements. These metrics typically include throughput, response time, resource utilization, and capacity limits, among others. Throughput, for example, measures the rate at which a system can process incoming requests or transactions, providing insights into its processing capacity:

bashCopy code

```
sar -q 1 10
```

This command, using the **sar** tool in Linux, displays the system's average load queue over a specific time interval, helping assess the system's processing capacity.

Response time, on the other hand, measures the time taken for a system to respond to user requests or transactions, indicating its responsiveness and efficiency:

bashCopy code

```
curl -o /dev/null -s -w "%{time_total}\n" http://example.com
```

This command, using **curl** in Linux, sends a request to the specified URL and measures the total time taken for the request, providing insights into the system's response time.

Resource utilization metrics, such as CPU usage, memory usage, and disk I/O, help assess the system's resource efficiency and capacity utilization:

bashCopy code

```
top
```

This command displays real-time information about CPU usage, memory usage, and other system metrics, allowing administrators to monitor resource utilization and identify potential bottlenecks.

Capacity limits, including maximum concurrent users, peak transaction rates, and data storage capacity, define the upper bounds of a system's scalability and help organizations plan for future growth:

bashCopy code

```
ulimit -u
```

This command displays the maximum number of user processes allowed per user, providing insights into the system's capacity limits in terms of concurrent users.

In addition to these core metrics, organizations may also consider secondary metrics such as latency, error rates, and queue lengths to gain a more comprehensive understanding of system performance and scalability. Latency measures the time taken for individual operations or transactions, providing insights into the system's responsiveness at the micro-level:

bashCopy code

```
ping -c 5 example.com
```

This command sends ICMP echo requests to the specified host and measures the round-trip latency, helping assess network latency and communication performance.

Error rates indicate the frequency of errors or failures encountered during system operations, highlighting potential reliability and scalability issues:

bashCopy code

```
tail -f /var/log/syslog | grep -i error
```

This command monitors system logs in real-time and filters for error messages, allowing administrators to track error rates and identify underlying issues impacting scalability.

Queue lengths, particularly in distributed systems or message queues, indicate the backlog of requests or tasks awaiting processing, providing insights into system congestion and scalability constraints:

bashCopy code

```
rabbitmqctl list_queues
```

This command, when used with RabbitMQ, lists all queues in the message broker along with their respective lengths, helping administrators monitor queue lengths and identify potential scalability issues.

Once organizations have established relevant scalability metrics, they need to establish baseline performance benchmarks and conduct regular performance testing to assess scalability under different conditions and workloads. Load testing tools such as Apache JMeter or Vegeta can be used to simulate concurrent user activity and measure system performance under varying levels of load:

bashCopy code

```
jmeter -n -t test_plan.jmx -l results.jtl
```

This command runs a JMeter test plan, simulating user activity specified in the test plan file and recording performance metrics in the results file.

Continuous monitoring and performance analysis are essential to track scalability metrics over time, identify performance degradation or bottlenecks, and proactively address scalability challenges as they arise. Monitoring tools such as Prometheus or Grafana can be deployed to collect and visualize scalability metrics in real-time:

bashCopy code

```
prometheus --config-file=prometheus.yml
```

This command starts the Prometheus server with the specified configuration file, allowing organizations to collect and store metrics from various sources for monitoring and analysis.

In summary, scalability metrics and measurement are critical components of assessing and improving system scalability in today's data-driven and dynamic business environments. By defining relevant metrics, establishing baseline benchmarks, conducting performance testing, and continuously monitoring system performance, organizations can identify scalability issues early, optimize system resources, and ensure that their systems can scale efficiently to meet evolving demands and growth opportunities.

Scalability challenges in modern applications are pervasive, given the ever-increasing demands for performance, reliability, and flexibility in today's dynamic digital landscape. As organizations strive to accommodate growing user bases, handle larger datasets, and support diverse workloads, they encounter various hurdles that impede their ability to scale effectively. These challenges span multiple dimensions, including architectural complexities, resource limitations, operational overhead, and technological constraints, each presenting unique obstacles that must be addressed to achieve seamless scalability.

One of the primary scalability challenges faced by modern applications is architectural complexity, stemming from the adoption of distributed and microservices-based architectures. While these architectural paradigms offer benefits such as modularity, flexibility, and fault isolation, they also introduce inherent complexities in managing inter-

service communication, orchestrating deployments, and ensuring consistency across distributed components. To mitigate these challenges, organizations often leverage container orchestration platforms such as Kubernetes:
bashCopy code

```
kubectl scale deployment <deployment-name> --replicas=<num-replicas>
```

This command, using Kubernetes, scales a deployment by adjusting the number of replicas to handle increased traffic or workload demands, facilitating horizontal scalability in distributed environments.

Moreover, modern applications must contend with resource limitations, including compute, storage, and network capacity, which can constrain their ability to scale effectively. As application workloads grow and evolve, resource contention and bottlenecks may arise, leading to degraded performance and diminished user experience. To address resource limitations, organizations employ techniques such as auto-scaling and resource optimization:
bashCopy code

```
aws autoscaling update-auto-scaling-group --auto-scaling-group-name <group-name> --min-size=<min-size> --max-size=<max-size>
```

This command, using AWS Auto Scaling, adjusts the minimum and maximum size of an auto-scaling group based on predefined thresholds, enabling applications to dynamically scale resources in response to changing workload demands.

Furthermore, operational overhead poses a significant scalability challenge for organizations managing complex application environments. As the number of services, dependencies, and configurations increases, so does the complexity of deployment, monitoring, and maintenance tasks. To streamline operations and reduce overhead, organizations implement infrastructure as code (IaC) practices and automation tools:

bashCopy code

```
terraform apply
```

This command, using Terraform, deploys and manages infrastructure resources defined in code, enabling organizations to automate provisioning and configuration tasks, minimize manual intervention, and enhance scalability and repeatability in deployment workflows.

Additionally, technological constraints, such as database scalability limitations, software bottlenecks, and integration challenges, present significant hurdles for scaling modern applications. Traditional relational databases, for example, may struggle to handle the volume and velocity of data in high-throughput environments, leading organizations to explore alternative database technologies such as NoSQL or NewSQL:

bashCopy code

```
cqlsh -u <username> -p <password> -f create_keyspace.cql
```

This command, using the Cassandra Query Language Shell (cqlsh), executes a script to create a new keyspace in Apache Cassandra, a distributed NoSQL database designed for high scalability and availability.

Moreover, ensuring data consistency and integrity across distributed systems poses a formidable scalability challenge, particularly in scenarios involving eventual consistency and multi-master replication. Organizations must implement strategies such as conflict resolution mechanisms, data partitioning, and distributed transactions to maintain consistency while scaling out their systems:

bashCopy code

```
etcdctl member add <member-name>
```

This command, using etcdctl for etcd, adds a new member to the etcd cluster, enabling organizations to scale out their distributed key-value store while ensuring data consistency and fault tolerance.

In summary, scalability challenges in modern applications are multifaceted and require comprehensive strategies and technologies to address effectively. By leveraging scalable architectural patterns, optimizing resource utilization, automating operational tasks, adopting suitable technologies, and ensuring data consistency, organizations can overcome these challenges and achieve seamless scalability to meet the evolving demands of their users and business operations.

Chapter 2: Horizontal and Vertical Scaling Techniques

Horizontal scaling, also known as scaling out, is a critical technique employed by organizations to meet increasing demand for their services and applications. This strategy involves adding more instances of the application across multiple machines or servers to distribute the workload and handle higher traffic volumes. Horizontal scaling is particularly advantageous as it enhances redundancy, improves fault tolerance, and enables seamless scalability without the constraints of individual hardware limitations. Implementing horizontal scaling effectively requires careful planning, architecture design, and deployment strategies tailored to the specific requirements and characteristics of the application.

One common approach to implementing horizontal scaling is through the use of containerization technologies such as Docker. Containers encapsulate applications and their dependencies, making it easy to deploy and manage multiple instances across different environments. The Docker CLI provides commands to create, run, and manage containers, facilitating horizontal scaling with minimal effort:

bashCopy code

```
docker run -d --name=my-container my-image
```

This command creates and runs a Docker container named "my-container" using the specified image, enabling organizations to quickly deploy additional instances of their application across multiple hosts or clusters.

Moreover, container orchestration platforms like Kubernetes offer robust tools for automating the deployment, scaling, and management of containerized applications at scale. Kubernetes abstracts the underlying infrastructure and provides a unified API for managing application deployments across clusters of machines. Organizations can leverage Kubernetes commands to scale deployments horizontally based on predefined metrics or policies:

bashCopy code

```
kubectl scale deployment my-deployment --replicas=3
```

This command scales a Kubernetes deployment named "my-deployment" to three replicas, ensuring that three instances of the application are running to handle increased workload demands.

Furthermore, cloud computing platforms such as Amazon Web Services (AWS) and Microsoft Azure offer scalable infrastructure services that enable organizations to provision and manage compute resources dynamically. With AWS Auto Scaling or Azure Autoscale, organizations can define scaling policies to automatically adjust the number of instances based on metrics such as CPU utilization or incoming traffic:

bashCopy code

```
aws autoscaling update-auto-scaling-group --auto-scaling-group-name my-group --min-size 2 --max-size 10 --desired-capacity 5
```

This AWS CLI command updates the auto-scaling group named "my-group" to have a minimum of two instances, a maximum of ten instances, and a desired capacity of five instances, ensuring that the application scales horizontally to meet changing demand.

In addition to containerization and cloud-based scaling, organizations can implement a microservices architecture to facilitate horizontal scaling of individual services within an application. Microservices decouple the application into smaller, independently deployable components, allowing teams to scale each service independently based on its specific resource needs and workload characteristics:

bashCopy code

```
docker-compose scale my-service=3
```

This command scales the Docker Compose service named "my-service" to three instances, demonstrating how microservices architecture enables granular horizontal scaling of individual components within an application.

Furthermore, organizations can leverage load balancers to distribute incoming traffic evenly across multiple instances of the application, ensuring high availability and efficient resource utilization. Load balancers such as NGINX or HAProxy monitor the health and performance of backend servers and route requests based on predefined algorithms or rules:

bashCopy code

```
kubectl expose deployment my-deployment --type=LoadBalancer --port=80 --target-port=8080
```

This command exposes a Kubernetes deployment named "my-deployment" as a load-balanced service on port 80, enabling external traffic to be distributed across multiple instances of the application.

Moreover, implementing horizontal scaling requires organizations to consider factors such as data consistency, session management, and distributed caching to ensure seamless operation across multiple instances. Techniques

such as database sharding, distributed caching with tools like Redis or Memcached, and stateless session management are essential for maintaining consistency and performance in horizontally scaled environments:
bashCopy code

```
redis-cli --cluster create <host>:<port> ... --cluster-replicas 1
```

This Redis command creates a Redis cluster with the specified master nodes and replica nodes, enabling organizations to distribute data across multiple instances for improved scalability and fault tolerance.

In summary, horizontal scaling implementation strategies are essential for organizations seeking to accommodate increasing demand and ensure high availability and performance of their applications. By leveraging containerization, cloud-based scaling, microservices architecture, load balancing, and other techniques, organizations can achieve seamless horizontal scalability, enabling their applications to handle growing workloads with ease.

Vertical scaling, also known as scaling up, is a crucial aspect of optimizing the performance and capacity of an application by increasing the resources of a single server or instance. Unlike horizontal scaling, which involves adding more instances to distribute the workload, vertical scaling focuses on enhancing the capabilities of individual servers to handle increased demands. This approach is particularly beneficial for applications with monolithic architectures or workloads that cannot be easily distributed across multiple instances. Implementing vertical scaling effectively requires adherence to best practices and careful consideration of factors such as resource allocation, performance tuning, and application architecture.

One of the primary considerations in vertical scaling is selecting the appropriate hardware components to support the increased resource requirements of the application. This may involve upgrading the CPU, RAM, storage, or network capacity of the server to accommodate higher workloads. Cloud service providers offer flexible options for vertically scaling virtual machines or instances to meet specific performance requirements:

bashCopy code

```
gcloud compute instances set-machine-type my-instance --machine-type n1-standard-8
```

This command, using Google Cloud Platform's gcloud CLI, changes the machine type of the specified instance "my-instance" to "n1-standard-8", providing it with eight virtual CPUs and ample memory for increased performance.

Moreover, optimizing the configuration of the operating system and runtime environment is essential for maximizing the efficiency of vertical scaling. This includes fine-tuning parameters such as kernel settings, resource limits, and caching mechanisms to ensure optimal utilization of available resources:

bashCopy code

```
sysctl -w vm.swappiness=10
```

This command adjusts the kernel parameter "vm.swappiness" to set the tendency of the Linux kernel to swap memory pages to disk, optimizing memory management for improved performance in vertical scaling scenarios.

Additionally, organizations must optimize their applications for vertical scaling by identifying and addressing performance bottlenecks and inefficiencies. This may involve profiling the application to identify CPU-intensive or memory-intensive tasks and optimizing algorithms or code paths to reduce resource consumption:

bashCopy code

gdb my-application

This command launches the GNU Debugger (GDB) to debug and profile the specified application "my-application", enabling developers to analyze its behavior and identify performance bottlenecks for optimization.

Furthermore, vertical scaling encompasses database optimization techniques to improve the performance and scalability of data storage and retrieval operations. This may include indexing frequently queried fields, partitioning large tables, or optimizing query execution plans to reduce latency and improve throughput:

bashCopy code

ALTER TABLE my_table ADD INDEX index_name (column_name);

This SQL command adds an index on the specified column "column_name" in the table "my_table", improving query performance by facilitating faster data retrieval operations.

Moreover, organizations can leverage caching mechanisms to offload compute-intensive or frequently accessed data from the database, reducing the workload on the underlying storage infrastructure:

bashCopy code

redis-cli SET my_key "my_value"

This Redis command stores a key-value pair "my_key" and "my_value" in the Redis cache, enabling organizations to cache frequently accessed data for faster retrieval and improved performance.

Additionally, implementing efficient resource utilization practices such as over-provisioning, dynamic resource allocation, and workload prioritization can help optimize the performance and scalability of vertically scaled environments:

bashCopy code

```
kubectl apply -f resource-limit.yaml
```

This Kubernetes command applies resource limits specified in the YAML file "resource-limit.yaml" to ensure that containers are allocated appropriate CPU and memory resources, preventing resource contention and ensuring consistent performance in vertically scaled deployments.

In summary, vertical scaling best practices are essential for organizations seeking to optimize the performance and scalability of their applications. By selecting appropriate hardware, optimizing operating system and runtime configurations, optimizing application code, tuning database performance, leveraging caching mechanisms, and implementing efficient resource utilization practices, organizations can effectively scale their applications vertically to meet growing demands and deliver superior user experiences.

Chapter 3: Load Balancing Strategies for Distributed Systems

Load balancers play a crucial role in distributing incoming network traffic across multiple servers to ensure high availability, reliability, and scalability of applications. There are several types of load balancers available, each designed to address specific use cases and deployment scenarios. Understanding the different types of load balancers and their selection criteria is essential for organizations to effectively manage their traffic and optimize application performance.

One of the most common types of load balancers is the Layer 4 load balancer, which operates at the transport layer (TCP/UDP) of the OSI model. Layer 4 load balancers route traffic based on IP address and port numbers, making forwarding decisions without inspecting the actual content of the packets. This type of load balancer is ideal for applications that require simple, fast, and efficient traffic distribution without the need for advanced application-aware features:

bashCopy code

```
aws elbv2 create-load-balancer --name my-load-balancer
--type network
```

This AWS CLI command creates a Layer 4 network load balancer named "my-load-balancer", which routes traffic based on IP addresses and ports.

Another common type of load balancer is the Layer 7 load balancer, which operates at the application layer (HTTP/HTTPS) of the OSI model. Layer 7 load balancers can inspect the content of the incoming requests, allowing for more intelligent routing decisions based on factors such as URL paths, HTTP headers, or cookies. This type of load balancer is suitable for applications that require advanced traffic management capabilities, such as content-based routing, request rewriting, or SSL termination:

bashCopy code

```
gcloud compute forwarding-rules create my-rule --load-balancing-scheme EXTERNAL --global --target-http-proxy my-proxy --port-range 80
```

This Google Cloud CLI command creates a Layer 7 HTTP(S) forwarding rule named "my-rule" to route incoming HTTP traffic to the specified target HTTP proxy.

Moreover, organizations can choose between hardware-based load balancers and software-based load balancers based on their performance, scalability, and cost requirements. Hardware load balancers are physical appliances that provide dedicated processing power and specialized hardware for handling high volumes of network traffic. They offer predictable performance and high throughput but may incur higher upfront costs and require additional maintenance:

bashCopy code

```
aws elbv2 create-load-balancer --name my-hardware-lb --type network --subnet public-subnet-1 --scheme internal
```

This AWS CLI command creates a hardware-based network load balancer named "my-hardware-lb" within the specified subnet and internal scheme.

Alternatively, software-based load balancers, also known as virtual load balancers, are deployed as virtual machines or containers within the organization's infrastructure.

They leverage commodity hardware and virtualization technologies to provide flexible and cost-effective load balancing solutions. Software load balancers offer scalability, agility, and ease of deployment but may have limitations in terms of performance and scalability compared to hardware appliances:

bashCopy code

```
kubectl apply -f my-nginx-ingress.yaml
```

This Kubernetes command deploys a software-based NGINX ingress controller as a Kubernetes resource using the YAML file "my-nginx-ingress.yaml", enabling organizations to leverage software load balancing capabilities within their Kubernetes clusters.

In addition to the type of load balancer, organizations must consider various selection criteria when choosing the right load balancer for their environment. These criteria include:

Performance: Evaluate the load balancer's throughput, latency, and connection handling capabilities to ensure it can handle the expected traffic volume and meet performance requirements.

Scalability: Assess the load balancer's ability to scale horizontally or vertically to accommodate increasing traffic demands without sacrificing performance or reliability.

High availability: Choose a load balancer that offers built-in redundancy, failover mechanisms, and geographic distribution to ensure continuous availability and resilience against failures.

Security: Consider the load balancer's support for SSL/TLS termination, encryption, authentication, and access control mechanisms to protect sensitive data and prevent security breaches.

Flexibility: Look for a load balancer that provides configurable routing policies, health checks, and traffic management features to support diverse application architectures and deployment scenarios.

Integration: Ensure compatibility with existing infrastructure, applications, and management tools to facilitate seamless integration and minimize deployment complexity.

Cost: Evaluate the total cost of ownership, including upfront licensing fees, ongoing maintenance costs, and scalability considerations, to determine the most cost-effective solution for the organization's budget and requirements.

By carefully evaluating these selection criteria and choosing the appropriate type of load balancer based on the organization's specific needs and objectives, organizations can effectively optimize their application delivery infrastructure, improve performance, and ensure seamless scalability and availability of their services.

Dynamic load balancing algorithms play a crucial role in optimizing the distribution of network traffic across multiple servers in real-time based on current system conditions and workload characteristics. These algorithms are essential for ensuring efficient resource utilization, minimizing response times, and enhancing the overall performance and reliability of distributed systems. There are several dynamic load balancing algorithms, each designed to address specific challenges and requirements in different deployment scenarios. Understanding the principles behind these algorithms and their deployment techniques is essential for organizations to effectively manage their traffic and optimize application performance.

One of the most commonly used dynamic load balancing algorithms is the Round Robin algorithm, which evenly distributes incoming requests across a pool of servers in a cyclic manner. This algorithm is simple to implement and ensures fair distribution of traffic among servers, making it suitable for basic load balancing scenarios:

bashCopy code

```
nginx.conf: upstream my_backend { server 192.168.1.101;
server 192.168.1.102; server 192.168.1.103; } location / {
proxy_pass http://my_backend; }
```

In this NGINX configuration, the Round Robin algorithm is implicitly used to distribute incoming requests among the servers listed in the upstream block.

Another widely used dynamic load balancing algorithm is the Least Connections algorithm, which directs incoming requests to the server with the fewest active connections. This algorithm aims to distribute traffic more evenly based on the current load on each server, effectively reducing response times and improving overall system performance:

bashCopy code

```
haproxy.conf: backend my_backend balance leastconn
server server1 192.168.1.101:80 check server server2
192.168.1.102:80 check server server3 192.168.1.103:80
check
```

In this HAProxy configuration, the Least Connections algorithm is specified in the "balance" directive to distribute incoming requests based on the number of active connections on each server.

Moreover, organizations can leverage dynamic load balancing algorithms such as Weighted Round Robin and IP Hash for more advanced traffic management and routing strategies. The Weighted Round Robin algorithm assigns a weight to each server based on its processing capacity or resource availability, allowing administrators to prioritize traffic distribution according to server capabilities:

bashCopy code

nginx.conf: upstream my_backend { server 192.168.1.101 weight=3; server 192.168.1.102 weight=2; server 192.168.1.103 weight=1; }

In this NGINX configuration, the Weighted Round Robin algorithm is used to assign higher weights to servers with higher processing capacities, influencing the distribution of incoming requests accordingly.

Similarly, the IP Hash algorithm calculates a hash value based on the client's IP address and uses it to determine the destination server for each request. This ensures that requests from the same client are consistently routed to the same server, which can be beneficial for session persistence or stateful applications:

bashCopy code

haproxy.conf: backend my_backend balance source server server1 192.168.1.101:80 check server server2 192.168.1.102:80 check server server3 192.168.1.103:80 check

In this HAProxy configuration, the IP Hash algorithm is specified using the "balance" directive with the "source" parameter, ensuring that requests from the same client are consistently directed to the same server.

Furthermore, organizations can implement more sophisticated dynamic load balancing algorithms such as Least Response Time, Adaptive Load Balancing, or Predictive Load Balancing to further optimize traffic distribution based on factors such as server response times, system resource utilization, or predictive analytics.

In summary, dynamic load balancing algorithms play a vital role in optimizing the distribution of network traffic across multiple servers to ensure high availability, reliability, and performance of distributed systems. By understanding the principles behind these algorithms and their deployment techniques, organizations can effectively manage their traffic, minimize response times, and enhance the scalability and resilience of their applications.

Chapter 4: Caching and Data Replication for Improved Performance

Cache invalidation strategies are crucial for maintaining data consistency and ensuring the accuracy of cached information in distributed systems. These strategies govern how cached data is invalidated or updated when the underlying data changes, preventing stale or outdated content from being served to users. Effective cache invalidation strategies are essential for improving application performance, reducing latency, and minimizing the risk of serving incorrect or obsolete data to users. There are several cache invalidation techniques and best practices that organizations can employ to optimize their caching systems and ensure data integrity.

One common cache invalidation strategy is the Time-to-Live (TTL) approach, which involves setting a predefined expiration time for cached data. In this approach, each cached item is associated with a TTL value that determines how long it remains valid before being automatically invalidated and refreshed from the source. TTL-based cache invalidation is simple to implement and offers a straightforward way to manage cache consistency:

bashCopy code

REDIS> SET mykey "myvalue" EX 3600

In this Redis CLI command, the "SET" command is used to store a key-value pair with an expiration time of 3600 seconds (1 hour).

Another cache invalidation strategy is the Write-Through caching approach, where updates or modifications to the

data are propagated directly to the cache and the underlying data store simultaneously. This ensures that the cached data is always synchronized with the source data, eliminating the need for explicit cache invalidation:
bashCopy code
AWS DAX: Automatically synchronizes cached data with the underlying Amazon DynamoDB table in real-time.

In Amazon DynamoDB Accelerator (DAX), write-through caching is automatically enabled, ensuring that updates made to the DynamoDB table are reflected in the cache in real-time.

Moreover, organizations can implement cache invalidation strategies based on event-driven invalidation mechanisms, where changes to the underlying data trigger cache invalidation events. This approach ensures that cached data is invalidated promptly whenever relevant data changes occur, maintaining cache consistency and data integrity:
bashCopy code
AWS CloudFront: Configure cache invalidation rules to invalidate cached objects based on specified events or criteria.

Using AWS CloudFront, organizations can define cache invalidation rules to automatically invalidate cached objects when changes are detected in the origin data source.

Additionally, cache invalidation strategies can leverage versioning or timestamping mechanisms to track changes to the underlying data and invalidate cached items accordingly. By associating each cached item with a version number or timestamp, cache systems can efficiently identify and invalidate outdated or stale data when updates occur:

bashCopy code

Memcached: Store version numbers or timestamps alongside cached data to track changes and invalidate outdated entries.

In Memcached, applications can store version numbers or timestamps as part of the cached data structure to facilitate efficient cache invalidation based on data changes.

Furthermore, organizations can implement manual cache invalidation techniques, where administrators or developers explicitly trigger cache invalidation operations based on predefined criteria or business logic. While manual cache invalidation provides fine-grained control over cache management, it requires additional effort and coordination to ensure timely and accurate invalidation of cached data:

bashCopy code

Varnish Cache: Use the "ban" command to manually invalidate cached objects based on custom criteria or patterns.

In Varnish Cache, administrators can issue the "ban" command with specific patterns or criteria to manually invalidate cached objects matching the specified conditions.

In summary, cache invalidation strategies are essential for maintaining data consistency and ensuring the accuracy of cached information in distributed systems. By implementing effective cache invalidation techniques such as TTL-based expiration, write-through caching, event-driven invalidation, versioning, or manual invalidation, organizations can optimize their caching systems, improve application performance, and deliver a seamless user experience. Cloud autoscaling policies and triggers play a pivotal role in optimizing resource utilization, enhancing performance, and ensuring cost-effectiveness in cloud-based environments. These policies and triggers enable automated scaling of computing resources based on predefined conditions, such as changes in workload demand, resource utilization metrics, or user-defined thresholds. By dynamically adjusting the capacity of cloud infrastructure in response to fluctuating demands, organizations can maintain optimal performance levels, minimize resource wastage, and meet service level agreements effectively. Deploying effective autoscaling policies and triggers requires careful planning, configuration, and monitoring to ensure seamless scalability and efficient resource management.

One of the key components of cloud autoscaling is defining scaling policies that dictate how and when to scale resources based on specific triggers or conditions. These policies typically include parameters such as minimum and maximum instance counts, scaling cooldown periods, and scaling step adjustments:

bashCopy code

AWS Auto Scaling: Create scaling policies using the AWS Management Console or AWS CLI with the "put-scaling-policy" command.

In AWS Auto Scaling, administrators can define scaling policies using the AWS Management Console or AWS CLI. For example, the "put-scaling-policy" command allows users to create scaling policies and specify parameters such as the scaling adjustment type, target resource, and scaling adjustment amount.

Moreover, organizations can utilize various scaling triggers to dynamically adjust resource capacity in response to changing workload patterns or performance metrics. Common triggers include CPU utilization, memory utilization, network traffic, and application-specific metrics:

bashCopy code

Azure Autoscale: Configure autoscaling rules in Azure using the Azure Portal or Azure CLI with the "az monitor autoscale" command.

In Azure Autoscale, administrators can configure autoscaling rules using the Azure Portal or Azure CLI. The "az monitor autoscale" command allows users to define autoscaling rules based on metrics such as CPU utilization, memory usage, or custom application metrics.

Furthermore, cloud providers offer advanced autoscaling capabilities that leverage machine learning algorithms and predictive analytics to anticipate workload patterns and proactively adjust resource capacity:

bashCopy code

Google Cloud Autoscaler: Enable predictive autoscaling in Google Cloud Platform (GCP) using the GCP Console or gcloud CLI with the "gcloud beta compute instance-groups managed set-autoscaling" command.

In Google Cloud Platform (GCP), administrators can enable predictive autoscaling using the GCP Console or gcloud CLI. The "gcloud beta compute instance-groups managed set-autoscaling" command allows users to configure autoscaling policies and enable predictive scaling based on historical workload patterns and predictive analytics.

Additionally, organizations can implement custom scaling policies and triggers tailored to their specific workload characteristics, business requirements, and performance objectives. Custom autoscaling solutions may involve integrating third-party monitoring tools, implementing custom scripts or plugins, or developing application-specific logic for triggering scaling events:

bashCopy code

Kubernetes Horizontal Pod Autoscaler (HPA): Define custom scaling policies in Kubernetes using the HorizontalPodAutoscaler resource manifest or kubectl CLI with the "kubectl autoscale" command.

In Kubernetes, administrators can define custom scaling policies using the HorizontalPodAutoscaler resource manifest or kubectl CLI. The "kubectl autoscale" command allows users to configure autoscaling for Kubernetes deployments based on CPU utilization or custom metrics.

Furthermore, continuous monitoring and optimization of autoscaling policies and triggers are essential to ensure effective resource management and cost optimization:

bashCopy code

AWS CloudWatch: Monitor and optimize autoscaling policies in AWS using CloudWatch metrics and alarms configured through the AWS Management Console or AWS CLI with the "put-metric-alarm" command.

In AWS, administrators can monitor and optimize autoscaling policies using CloudWatch metrics and alarms configured through the AWS Management Console or AWS CLI. The "put-metric-alarm" command enables users to create alarms based on various metrics to trigger autoscaling actions. In summary, cloud autoscaling policies and triggers are critical for dynamically adjusting resource capacity in response to changing workload demands and performance metrics. By defining appropriate scaling policies, configuring triggers, leveraging advanced autoscaling capabilities, and continuously monitoring and optimizing resource utilization, organizations can achieve optimal performance, scalability, and cost efficiency in cloud environments.

Chapter 5: Elasticity and Auto-scaling in Cloud Environments

Elastic Load Balancing (ELB) is a critical component in cloud infrastructure, designed to distribute incoming traffic across multiple targets, such as EC2 instances, containers, or IP addresses, to ensure high availability and fault tolerance. Configuring Elastic Load Balancing involves several parameters and settings to optimize performance, scalability, and reliability. AWS provides several types of Elastic Load Balancers, including Classic Load Balancer, Application Load Balancer, and Network Load Balancer, each offering specific features and functionalities tailored to different use cases.

To configure Elastic Load Balancing in AWS, administrators typically start by selecting the appropriate load balancer type based on their requirements and the nature of their workload. For example, the Application Load Balancer (ALB) is ideal for routing HTTP/HTTPS traffic to multiple targets, while the Network Load Balancer (NLB) excels in handling TCP/UDP traffic with ultra-low latency.

bashCopy code

```
aws elbv2 create-load-balancer --name my-application-load-balancer --type application --subnets subnet-1234567890abcdef0 subnet-0987654321abcdef1
```

In this AWS CLI command, the "create-load-balancer" operation is used to create an Application Load Balancer named "my-application-load-balancer" in the specified subnets.

Once the load balancer type is selected, administrators configure listeners and target groups to define how incoming traffic is distributed and routed to the backend targets. Listeners define the protocol and port on which the load balancer listens for incoming traffic, while target groups specify the destination targets and health check settings.

bashCopy code

```
aws elbv2 create-listener --load-balancer-arn my-load-balancer-arn --protocol HTTP --port 80 --default-actions Type=forward,TargetGroupArn=target-group-arn
```

In this CLI command, the "create-listener" operation is used to create an HTTP listener on port 80 for the specified load balancer, forwarding traffic to the target group identified by its ARN.

Moreover, administrators configure health checks to monitor the health and status of the registered targets and automatically route traffic only to healthy instances. Health checks periodically evaluate the health of each target based on configurable criteria such as HTTP status codes, response times, or custom endpoint checks.

bashCopy code

```
aws elbv2 create-target-group --name my-target-group --protocol HTTP --port 80 --vpc-id vpc-1234567890abcdef0 --health-check-protocol HTTP --health-check-path /health --health-check-interval-seconds 30 --health-check-timeout-seconds 5 --healthy-threshold-count 2 --unhealthy-threshold-count 2
```

This CLI command creates a target group named "my-target-group" for HTTP traffic on port 80, specifying a health check endpoint "/health" with a 30-second interval,

5-second timeout, and thresholds for determining target health.

Additionally, administrators can configure advanced settings such as cross-zone load balancing, connection draining, sticky sessions, SSL termination, and access logs to customize the behavior and performance of the load balancer based on specific requirements and use cases.

bashCopy code

```
aws elbv2 modify-load-balancer-attributes --load-balancer-arn my-load-balancer-arn --attributes Key=access_logs.s3.enabled,Value=true
Key=access_logs.s3.bucket,Value=my-s3-bucket
Key=access_logs.s3.prefix,Value=my-prefix
```

This CLI command modifies the attributes of the specified load balancer to enable access logs and specify the S3 bucket and prefix for storing log files.

Furthermore, administrators can use CloudWatch metrics and alarms to monitor the performance and health of Elastic Load Balancers and trigger autoscaling actions based on predefined thresholds or metrics such as request count, latency, or error rates.

bashCopy code

```
aws cloudwatch put-metric-alarm --alarm-name my-alarm --alarm-description "High Latency Alarm" --namespace AWS/ApplicationELB --metric-name TargetResponseTime --dimensions Name=LoadBalancer,Value=my-load-balancer-arn --statistic Average --period 60 --threshold 0.5 --comparison-operator GreaterThanThreshold --evaluation-periods 1 --alarm-actions arn:aws:autoscaling:us-east-
```

1:123456789012:autoScalingGroup:6d04d01c-b2ff-406a-b6d8-5dfEXAMPLE

In this CLI command, an alarm is created in CloudWatch to monitor the average response time of targets behind the specified load balancer, triggering autoscaling actions if the response time exceeds 0.5 seconds.

In summary, configuring Elastic Load Balancing involves defining listeners, target groups, health checks, and advanced settings to distribute incoming traffic efficiently, ensure high availability, and optimize performance in cloud environments. By leveraging the AWS CLI and CloudWatch metrics, administrators can automate the configuration process and monitor the health and performance of load balancers, enabling dynamic scaling and efficient resource utilization to meet changing workload demands.

Elastic Load Balancing (ELB) is a fundamental component in modern cloud architectures, designed to efficiently distribute incoming traffic across multiple targets, ensuring high availability, fault tolerance, and scalability. Configuring Elastic Load Balancing involves several crucial steps and settings to optimize performance, reliability, and security.

To begin configuring Elastic Load Balancing in AWS, one typically starts by selecting the appropriate load balancer type based on the specific requirements and characteristics of the workload. AWS offers several types of Elastic Load Balancers, including Classic Load Balancer, Application Load Balancer (ALB), and Network Load Balancer (NLB), each tailored to different use cases and traffic handling needs.

bashCopy code

```
aws elbv2 create-load-balancer --name my-application-
load-balancer --type application --subnets subnet-
1234567890abcdef0 subnet-0987654321abcdef1
```

This AWS CLI command creates an Application Load Balancer named "my-application-load-balancer" in the specified subnets.

Once the load balancer type is selected, administrators proceed to configure listeners and target groups. Listeners define the protocol and port on which the load balancer listens for incoming traffic, while target groups specify the destination targets and health check settings.

bashCopy code

```
aws elbv2 create-listener --load-balancer-arn my-load-
balancer-arn --protocol HTTP --port 80 --default-actions
Type=forward,TargetGroupArn=target-group-arn
```

In this CLI command, an HTTP listener on port 80 is created for the specified load balancer, forwarding traffic to the target group identified by its ARN.

Administrators then configure health checks to monitor the health and status of the registered targets and automatically route traffic only to healthy instances. Health checks periodically evaluate the health of each target based on configurable criteria such as HTTP status codes, response times, or custom endpoint checks.

bashCopy code

```
aws elbv2 create-target-group --name my-target-group --
protocol HTTP --port 80 --vpc-id vpc-1234567890abcdef0
--health-check-protocol HTTP --health-check-path /health
--health-check-interval-seconds 30 --health-check-
```

timeout-seconds 5 --healthy-threshold-count 2 -- unhealthy-threshold-count 2

This CLI command creates a target group for HTTP traffic on port 80, specifying a health check endpoint "/health" with a 30-second interval, 5-second timeout, and thresholds for determining target health.

Additionally, administrators can configure advanced settings such as cross-zone load balancing, connection draining, sticky sessions, SSL termination, and access logs to customize the behavior and performance of the load balancer based on specific requirements and use cases.

bashCopy code

```
aws elbv2 modify-load-balancer-attributes --load-balancer-arn my-load-balancer-arn --attributes Key=access_logs.s3.enabled,Value=true
Key=access_logs.s3.bucket,Value=my-s3-bucket
Key=access_logs.s3.prefix,Value=my-prefix
```

In this CLI command, the attributes of the specified load balancer are modified to enable access logs and specify the S3 bucket and prefix for storing log files.

Furthermore, administrators can utilize CloudWatch metrics and alarms to monitor the performance and health of Elastic Load Balancers and trigger autoscaling actions based on predefined thresholds or metrics such as request count, latency, or error rates.

bashCopy code

```
aws cloudwatch put-metric-alarm --alarm-name my-alarm --alarm-description "High Latency Alarm" --namespace AWS/ApplicationELB --metric-name TargetResponseTime --dimensions Name=LoadBalancer,Value=my-load-
```

balancer-arn --statistic Average --period 60 --threshold 0.5 --comparison-operator GreaterThanThreshold --evaluation-periods 1 --alarm-actions arn:aws:autoscaling:us-east-1:123456789012:autoScalingGroup:6d04d01c-b2ff-406a-b6d8-5dfEXAMPLE

In this CLI command, an alarm is created in CloudWatch to monitor the average response time of targets behind the specified load balancer, triggering autoscaling actions if the response time exceeds 0.5 seconds.

In summary, configuring Elastic Load Balancing involves defining listeners, target groups, health checks, and advanced settings to efficiently distribute incoming traffic, ensure high availability, and optimize performance in cloud environments. By leveraging the AWS CLI and CloudWatch metrics, administrators can automate the configuration process and monitor the health and performance of load balancers, enabling dynamic scaling and efficient resource utilization to meet changing workload demands.

Chapter 6: Database Sharding and Partitioning

Sharding techniques in relational databases play a crucial role in addressing scalability challenges by distributing data across multiple shards or partitions, thereby enabling horizontal scaling and improving performance. Sharding involves dividing a large dataset into smaller, more manageable segments called shards and distributing these shards across multiple database nodes. By spreading the workload across multiple nodes, sharding allows databases to handle larger volumes of data and accommodate growing numbers of users or transactions without sacrificing performance or availability.

To implement sharding in a relational database, administrators typically start by selecting a suitable sharding key, which is used to determine how data is partitioned across shards. The sharding key should be carefully chosen based on the access patterns and distribution characteristics of the data to ensure balanced shard distribution and efficient query execution.

```bash
bashCopy code
CREATE TABLE orders ( order_id INT PRIMARY KEY, customer_id INT, order_date DATE, ... ) PARTITION BY RANGE (order_date)( PARTITION p1 VALUES LESS THAN ('2022-01-01'), PARTITION p2 VALUES LESS THAN ('2023-01-01'), ... );
```

In MySQL, for example, administrators can create partitioned tables using the **PARTITION BY RANGE** clause and specifying the partitioning key (e.g., **order_date**) along with the partition boundaries.

Once the sharding key is defined, administrators can partition the database tables and distribute the data across multiple shards based on the selected key. Each shard typically contains a subset of the dataset, and data distribution strategies vary depending on factors such as data skew, query patterns, and availability requirements.

bashCopy code

```
ALTER TABLE orders ADD PARTITION ( PARTITION p3
VALUES LESS THAN ('2024-01-01') );
```

In MySQL, adding a new partition to an existing partitioned table can be achieved using the **ALTER TABLE** statement with the **ADD PARTITION** clause, specifying the new partition and its boundary.

To ensure data consistency and maintain referential integrity across shards, administrators may implement distributed transactions or use techniques such as two-phase commit (2PC) or three-phase commit (3PC) protocols.

bashCopy code

```
BEGIN; INSERT INTO orders (order_id, customer_id,
order_date) VALUES (1001, 123, '2024-02-21'); COMMIT;
```

In PostgreSQL, administrators can use standard SQL transactions to ensure atomicity and consistency across distributed database operations. By enclosing multiple SQL statements within a **BEGIN** and **COMMIT** block, administrators can ensure that all operations either succeed or fail together, preserving data integrity.

Additionally, administrators must consider data rebalancing and redistribution mechanisms to handle changes in data distribution patterns or shard capacities dynamically. Techniques such as range-based or hash-based sharding, dynamic partitioning, and automatic shard migration can help maintain balanced data distribution and optimize resource utilization across shards.

bashCopy code

```
ALTER TABLE orders REORGANIZE PARTITION;
```

In MySQL, the **ALTER TABLE** statement with the **REORGANIZE PARTITION** clause can be used to rebalance partitions and redistribute data across shards based on updated partitioning criteria or distribution requirements.

Furthermore, monitoring and managing sharded databases require specialized tools and techniques to track shard health, performance metrics, and query distribution patterns. Administrators may leverage database management systems (DBMS) with built-in sharding support or deploy third-party monitoring solutions to monitor shard status, identify performance bottlenecks, and troubleshoot issues.

In summary, sharding techniques in relational databases offer a scalable solution for handling large volumes of data and high transaction loads by distributing data across multiple shards. By carefully selecting sharding keys, implementing data distribution strategies, ensuring data consistency, and employing dynamic management and monitoring techniques, organizations can effectively leverage sharding to achieve scalability, performance, and availability goals in relational database environments.

Partitioning strategies in NoSQL databases are essential for distributing data across multiple nodes to achieve scalability, performance, and fault tolerance in distributed environments. NoSQL databases, such as MongoDB, Cassandra, and Amazon DynamoDB, utilize partitioning to horizontally scale data storage and processing capabilities, allowing them to handle large volumes of data and high transaction rates effectively.

In MongoDB, partitioning is achieved through sharding, where data is divided into smaller chunks called shards and distributed across multiple nodes in a cluster. MongoDB provides a built-in sharding feature that allows administrators to define sharding keys and configure sharded clusters to automatically distribute data based on these keys.

bashCopy code

```
sh.enableSharding("<database>");
db.<collection>.createIndex({ "<shardingKey>": 1 });
sh.shardCollection("<database>.<collection>", { "<shardingKey>": "hashed" });
```

To enable sharding in MongoDB, administrators first need to enable sharding for a specific database using the **sh.enableSharding()** command. Then, they create an index on the chosen sharding key using the **createIndex()** method. Finally, they shard the collection based on the sharding key using the **sh.shardCollection()** method, specifying whether to use a hashed or ranged sharding strategy.

Similarly, Apache Cassandra employs partitioning to distribute data across multiple nodes in a cluster using consistent hashing. Cassandra partitions data into smaller units called partitions and distributes these partitions across nodes based on the partition key. Cassandra's partitioning strategy ensures that data is evenly distributed across nodes, thereby achieving uniform workload distribution and efficient data access.

bashCopy code

```
CREATE    TABLE    <table_name>    (    <partition_key>
<data_type>,    ...    PRIMARY    KEY    (<partition_key>,
<clustering_column>)    )    WITH
<partitioning_and_clustering_options>;
```

In Cassandra, administrators define partitioning and
clustering keys when creating tables. The partition key
determines the distribution of data across nodes, while
the clustering columns define the order of data within
each partition. By carefully selecting partitioning and
clustering keys, administrators can optimize data
distribution and access patterns to improve performance
and scalability.

Amazon DynamoDB, a fully managed NoSQL database
service, also utilizes partitioning to distribute data across
multiple partitions in a highly available and scalable
manner. DynamoDB automatically partitions data based
on the primary key specified by the user when creating
tables. Each partition in DynamoDB is stored on multiple
servers to ensure fault tolerance and high availability.

bashCopy code

```
aws dynamodb create-table \ --table-name <table_name>
\                --attribute-definitions                \
AttributeName=<partition_key>,AttributeType=<data_typ
e>                \                --key-schema                \
AttributeName=<partition_key>,KeyType=HASH    \    --
billing-mode <billing_mode> \ --provisioned-throughput \
ReadCapacityUnits=<read_capacity_units>,WriteCapacity
Units=<write_capacity_units>
```

To create a table in DynamoDB, administrators use the
aws dynamodb create-table command, specifying the

table name, partition key, data type, and other configuration options such as billing mode and provisioned throughput capacity. DynamoDB automatically handles partitioning and distribution of data across partitions based on the specified primary key.

In summary, partitioning strategies in NoSQL databases are crucial for achieving scalability, performance, and fault tolerance in distributed environments. Whether through sharding in MongoDB, consistent hashing in Apache Cassandra, or automatic partitioning in Amazon DynamoDB, NoSQL databases leverage partitioning to distribute data across multiple nodes effectively. By understanding and implementing appropriate partitioning strategies, administrators can optimize data distribution, access patterns, and resource utilization to meet the scalability and performance requirements of their applications.

Chapter 7: Asynchronous Processing for Handling Bursty Workloads

Event-driven architecture (EDA) patterns are a fundamental aspect of modern distributed systems, providing a flexible and scalable approach to designing software systems. EDA revolves around the concept of events, which represent significant occurrences or changes in a system and drive the flow of data and control. Events can originate from various sources, including user interactions, system processes, external services, or sensors, and can trigger actions or workflows in response. By decoupling components and leveraging asynchronous communication, EDA enables systems to be more resilient, responsive, and adaptable to changing requirements and environments.

One of the key patterns in event-driven architecture is the event sourcing pattern, which involves capturing all changes to an application's state as a sequence of immutable events. Rather than storing the current state of an entity, event sourcing maintains a log of events that represent state transitions over time. This pattern provides a comprehensive audit trail of all changes, enabling features such as event replay, temporal querying, and deterministic state reconstruction. Event sourcing is particularly beneficial for systems requiring strong auditability, temporal querying capabilities, or support for complex business workflows.

bashCopy code

```
docker run -d --name eventstore -p 2113:2113 -p
1113:1113 eventstore/eventstore
```
To implement event sourcing, developers can utilize specialized event sourcing databases like EventStoreDB or Apache Kafka. For instance, deploying EventStoreDB can be achieved using Docker, as shown in the command above, which pulls the EventStoreDB Docker image and runs it as a container. Once deployed, applications can interact with the event store to append new events, query historical events, or subscribe to event streams for real-time processing.

Another essential pattern in event-driven architecture is the publish-subscribe pattern, which facilitates loose coupling between producers and consumers of events. In a publish-subscribe model, producers (publishers) generate events and publish them to a message broker or event bus, while consumers (subscribers) subscribe to specific types of events and receive notifications when those events occur. This decoupled communication model enables horizontal scalability, fault isolation, and dynamic extensibility of systems.

bashCopy code

```
kubectl apply -f kafka-cluster.yaml
```
To implement the publish-subscribe pattern, organizations commonly deploy message brokers or event streaming platforms like Apache Kafka. The command above demonstrates deploying a Kafka cluster using Kubernetes, where a YAML configuration file (kafka-cluster.yaml) defines the desired state of the Kafka cluster. Kubernetes automatically orchestrates

the deployment of Kafka brokers across multiple nodes, providing fault tolerance and scalability.

Additionally, the event-driven architecture embraces the choreography and orchestration patterns to coordinate the processing of events and manage complex workflows. Choreography emphasizes decentralized coordination, where individual services collaborate by reacting to events and emitting new events based on their internal logic. In contrast, orchestration centralizes control in a dedicated orchestrator or workflow engine, which coordinates the execution of activities and services in a predefined sequence.

```bash
bashCopy code
docker run -d --name cadence -p 7933:7933 -p 7934:7934 ubercadence/server:latest
```

To implement workflow orchestration, developers can use workflow orchestration engines like Cadence (by Uber). The command above demonstrates deploying the Cadence server using Docker, where the Cadence server image is pulled and run as a container. Once deployed, organizations can define and execute complex workflows using Cadence's domain-specific language and workflow engine, enabling coordination and management of distributed business processes.

Moreover, the event-driven architecture promotes the use of event-driven integration patterns to facilitate seamless communication and integration between disparate systems and services. Integration patterns such as event sourcing, command query responsibility segregation (CQRS), event-driven messaging, and event-driven collaboration enable organizations to build resilient, scalable, and adaptable integration solutions that meet the demands of modern distributed environments.

In summary, event-driven architecture patterns offer a powerful paradigm for designing scalable, resilient, and adaptable software systems. By leveraging patterns such as event sourcing, publish-subscribe, choreography, orchestration, and event-driven integration, organizations can build event-driven systems that efficiently process and respond to events, enabling real-time insights, dynamic workflows, and seamless integration across heterogeneous environments. Whether deploying specialized event sourcing databases, message brokers, workflow engines, or integration platforms, organizations can harness the capabilities of event-driven architecture to drive innovation and agility in their software development practices.

Message queuing systems play a crucial role in modern software architecture, facilitating asynchronous communication and decoupling of components within distributed systems. These systems enable applications to exchange messages reliably and efficiently, even in the face of varying processing speeds and system failures. By decoupling producers and consumers of messages, message queuing systems promote scalability, fault tolerance, and flexibility in system design.

One of the most popular message queuing systems is Apache Kafka, which is known for its high throughput, fault tolerance, and scalability. Kafka uses a distributed commit log architecture, where messages are stored durably on disk and replicated across multiple brokers for fault tolerance. Producers publish messages to Kafka topics, while consumers subscribe to these topics and process messages at their own pace. Kafka's distributed nature allows it to handle large volumes of data and support real-time stream processing use cases.

bashCopy code

```
wget https://downloads.apache.org/kafka/3.0.0/kafka_2.13-3.0.0.tgz tar -xzf kafka_2.13-3.0.0.tgz cd kafka_2.13-3.0.0
```

To deploy Kafka locally, you can download the Kafka distribution, extract it using the tar command, and navigate to the Kafka directory. From there, you can start a single-node Kafka broker using the following command:

bashCopy code

```
bin/kafka-server-start.sh config/server.properties
```

Once Kafka is running, you can create topics using the kafka-topics.sh command-line tool, produce messages to topics using the kafka-console-producer.sh tool, and consume messages from topics using the kafka-console-consumer.sh tool.

Another popular message queuing system is RabbitMQ, an open-source message broker that implements the Advanced Message Queuing Protocol (AMQP).

RabbitMQ supports various messaging patterns, including point-to-point, publish-subscribe, and request-reply. It offers features such as message acknowledgments, message routing, and message durability, making it suitable for building robust and reliable messaging systems.

bashCopy code

docker run -d --name rabbitmq -p 5672:5672 -p 15672:15672 rabbitmq:management

To deploy RabbitMQ using Docker, you can run the command above, which starts a RabbitMQ container with the management plugin enabled. This plugin provides a web-based user interface for monitoring and managing RabbitMQ instances. Once RabbitMQ is running, you can use the RabbitMQ management console or command-line tools to configure exchanges, queues, and bindings, as well as publish and consume messages.

In addition to Kafka and RabbitMQ, there are other message queuing systems available, each with its own features and strengths. For example, Apache ActiveMQ, NATS, Amazon SQS, and Microsoft Azure Service Bus are widely used in various use cases ranging from enterprise messaging to cloud-native application development.

bashCopy code

docker run -d --name activemq -p 61616:61616 -p 8161:8161 rmohr/activemq:latest

To deploy Apache ActiveMQ using Docker, you can use the command above, which starts an ActiveMQ container. ActiveMQ provides support for multiple messaging protocols, including AMQP, MQTT, and STOMP, and offers features such as message persistence, message selectors, and message expiration. In summary, message queuing systems are essential components of modern software architecture, enabling asynchronous communication and decoupling of components within distributed systems. Whether deploying Kafka for real-time event streaming, RabbitMQ for reliable message delivery, or ActiveMQ for enterprise messaging, organizations can leverage message queuing systems to build scalable, resilient, and flexible messaging solutions. With the ability to handle large volumes of data, support various messaging patterns, and integrate with diverse technologies, message queuing systems empower developers to design and deploy robust and efficient distributed systems.

Chapter 8: Scalable Data Storage Solutions

Distributed file systems (DFS) revolutionize data storage and management in large-scale computing environments by distributing file storage across multiple servers and providing a unified view of files to users and applications. DFS serves as a fundamental building block for distributed computing, enabling efficient and reliable data storage, access, and processing across distributed clusters. One of the most well-known distributed file systems is the Hadoop Distributed File System (HDFS), designed to handle large volumes of data across clusters of commodity hardware. HDFS divides files into blocks and replicates them across multiple DataNodes to ensure fault tolerance and data durability. To deploy HDFS, one can use the Apache Hadoop distribution and configure it using XML configuration files and shell commands.

```
bashCopy code
wget
https://downloads.apache.org/hadoop/common/hado
op-3.3.1/hadoop-3.3.1.tar.gz    tar    -xzf    hadoop-
3.3.1.tar.gz cd hadoop-3.3.1
```

To start an HDFS cluster, one can initialize the HDFS filesystem and start the NameNode and DataNode daemons using the following commands:

```
bashCopy code
bin/hdfs namenode -format sbin/start-dfs.sh
```

After starting the HDFS cluster, users can interact with the distributed file system using the Hadoop command-line interface (CLI) tools, such as **hdfs dfs** commands. These commands allow users to perform various operations on files and directories in the distributed file system, such as creating, deleting, copying, and listing files.

Another popular distributed file system is the Google File System (GFS), developed by Google to handle the vast amounts of data generated by its services. GFS employs a master-slave architecture with a single Master server coordinating multiple ChunkServers. It provides a scalable and fault-tolerant storage solution for Google's distributed computing infrastructure. While GFS is not directly available for public use, its design principles have influenced the development of other distributed file systems, including HDFS.

Similarly, the Amazon Simple Storage Service (S3) is a widely used object storage service provided by Amazon Web Services (AWS). While not strictly a distributed file system, S3 offers a highly scalable and durable storage solution for storing and retrieving any amount of data. Users can interact with S3 using the AWS Management Console, SDKs, or command-line tools such as the AWS Command Line Interface (CLI). To upload a file to an S3 bucket using the AWS CLI, one can use the **aws s3 cp** command:

bashCopy code

```
aws s3 cp local-file.txt s3://bucket-name/path/to/destination
```

Distributed file systems play a crucial role in distributed computing environments by enabling efficient storage and retrieval of large volumes of data across distributed clusters. By distributing data across multiple nodes and replicating it for fault tolerance, DFS ensures high availability and reliability of data. Moreover, DFS provides a unified namespace and transparent access to files, allowing applications to access data as if it were stored locally. With the advent of cloud computing and big data technologies, distributed file systems have become indispensable components of modern data infrastructure, powering a wide range of applications and services across industries.

Object storage systems have emerged as a key technology for achieving scalability in modern data environments, providing a highly scalable and cost-effective solution for storing vast amounts of unstructured data. Unlike traditional file systems, which organize data into hierarchical directory structures, object storage systems organize data as objects within a flat namespace. This approach simplifies data management and enables seamless scalability, as objects can be distributed across multiple nodes in a cluster without the need for a centralized metadata server. One of the most popular object storage systems is Amazon Simple Storage Service (S3), which offers a scalable, durable, and highly available storage solution for a wide range of use cases. To interact with S3 using the AWS CLI, users can use commands such as **aws s3 cp** to copy files to and from S3 buckets, **aws s3 ls** to list objects in a bucket, and **aws s3 rm** to delete objects from a bucket.

bashCopy code

```
aws s3 cp local-file.txt s3://bucket-name/path/to/destination
```

Another widely used object storage system is Azure Blob Storage, provided by Microsoft Azure. Azure Blob Storage offers scalable storage for objects, such as documents, images, videos, and application backups, and provides various tiers to optimize costs based on access frequency and durability requirements. Users can interact with Azure Blob Storage using the Azure CLI, PowerShell, or Azure Storage Explorer. For example, to upload a file to an Azure Blob Storage container using the Azure CLI, one can use the **az storage blob upload** command:

bashCopy code

```
az storage blob upload --file local-file.txt --container-name container-name --name destination/path/to/blob
```

Google Cloud Storage (GCS) is another popular object storage service that provides scalable and durable storage for objects of any size. GCS offers various storage classes to optimize costs based on data access patterns and retention requirements, including Standard, Nearline, and Coldline storage classes. Users can interact with GCS using the Google Cloud SDK or the Google Cloud Console. To upload a file to a GCS bucket using the **gsutil** command-line tool, one can use the following command:

bashCopy code

```
gsutil        cp        local-file.txt        gs://bucket-
name/path/to/destination
```

Object storage systems offer several advantages over traditional file systems, including scalability, durability, and cost-effectiveness. By decoupling data from the underlying storage infrastructure and providing a unified namespace for accessing objects, object storage systems enable organizations to manage petabytes of data efficiently and cost-effectively. Moreover, object storage systems support various data access protocols, such as HTTP, RESTful APIs, and SDKs, making it easy to integrate with modern applications and services. With the growing volume of unstructured data generated by IoT devices, social media platforms, and multimedia content, object storage systems have become essential components of modern data architectures, enabling organizations to store, manage, and analyze massive amounts of data at scale.

Chapter 9: High Availability Architectures for Resilience

Active-active and active-passive failover architectures are two common strategies used in designing highly available systems to minimize downtime and ensure continuous operation in the event of a failure. In an active-active architecture, multiple instances of a service or application are actively serving traffic simultaneously, distributing the workload across all instances. This setup enhances scalability and fault tolerance, as each instance is capable of handling requests independently, and traffic can be load-balanced across all active instances to optimize resource utilization and improve performance. Amazon Web Services (AWS) provides various services and features to implement active-active architectures, such as Amazon Route 53 for DNS-based load balancing, Amazon Elastic Load Balancing (ELB) for distributing incoming traffic across multiple EC2 instances, and Amazon RDS Multi-AZ deployment for database redundancy. With AWS CLI, users can create an active-active setup using these services by issuing commands such as **aws elb create-load-balancer** to create an Elastic Load Balancer, **aws rds create-db-instance** to create a Multi-AZ database instance, and **aws route53 change-resource-record-sets** to configure DNS records for routing traffic to the load balancer.

bashCopy code

```
aws elb create-load-balancer --load-balancer-name my-
load-balancer                           --listeners
"Protocol=HTTP,LoadBalancerPort=80,InstanceProtocol
=HTTP,InstancePort=80" --availability-zones us-west-1a
us-west-1b us-west-1c
```

On the other hand, in an active-passive architecture, only one instance, known as the primary or active node, handles incoming requests and processes data, while the standby or passive node remains idle until a failover event occurs. The standby node continuously monitors the primary node's health and automatically takes over its responsibilities when it detects a failure. This approach provides a cost-effective solution for achieving high availability, as resources are only provisioned and consumed when needed. However, the failover process may introduce some downtime, depending on the time required for the passive node to assume control and start serving traffic. To implement an active-passive failover architecture on AWS, users can leverage services like Amazon Route 53 for DNS failover, Amazon RDS Multi-AZ deployment for database redundancy, and AWS Lambda for automated failover orchestration. With AWS CLI, users can configure DNS failover using Route 53 by executing commands such as **aws route53 create-health-check** to create health checks for monitoring endpoint health and **aws route53 change-resource-record-sets** to update DNS records based on health check status.

bashCopy code

```
aws route53 create-health-check --caller-reference my-
health-check-1                    --health-check-config
"IPAddress=192.0.2.1,Port=80,Type=HTTP"
```

Overall, active-active and active-passive failover architectures are essential strategies for achieving high availability and fault tolerance in distributed systems. While active-active architectures offer superior scalability and performance by distributing workload across multiple instances, active-passive architectures provide a cost-effective solution with minimal management overhead. By leveraging cloud services and automation tools, organizations can implement robust failover architectures to ensure uninterrupted service delivery and mitigate the impact of failures on their operations.

Disaster recovery planning and implementation are crucial components of any organization's IT strategy, aimed at minimizing the impact of disruptive events such as natural disasters, cyber-attacks, or hardware failures on business operations. A comprehensive disaster recovery plan encompasses policies, procedures, and technologies designed to ensure the swift recovery of critical systems and data in the event of a disaster. The first step in disaster recovery planning is conducting a thorough risk assessment to identify potential threats and vulnerabilities that could jeopardize business continuity. Organizations can use tools like AWS CLI to assess their infrastructure's resilience by performing vulnerability scans and security assessments on their cloud resources.

bashCopy code

```
aws inspector start-assessment-run --assessment-template-arn arn:aws:inspector:us-west-2:123456789012:target/0-0kFIPusq/template/0-0kFIPusq
```

Once risks are identified, organizations can develop a disaster recovery strategy that outlines specific measures to mitigate these risks and ensure prompt recovery in case of a disaster. This strategy typically includes provisions for data backup and replication, redundant infrastructure deployment, and failover mechanisms. AWS CLI provides a range of commands to facilitate data backup and replication tasks using services like Amazon S3 for object storage and AWS Backup for automated backup management.

bashCopy code

```
aws s3 sync /local/directory s3://bucket-name
```

Moreover, organizations should establish clear roles and responsibilities for disaster recovery personnel and define communication protocols to ensure seamless coordination during a crisis. Regular testing and validation of the disaster recovery plan are essential to verify its effectiveness and identify any gaps or deficiencies that need to be addressed. AWS CLI offers commands to simulate disaster recovery scenarios and test failover procedures, such as creating Amazon CloudWatch alarms to trigger automated responses or initiating failover processes using AWS Lambda functions.

bashCopy code

```
aws cloudwatch put-metric-alarm --alarm-name my-
alarm --metric-name CPUUtilization --namespace
AWS/EC2 --statistic Average --period 300 --threshold 70
--comparison-operator
GreaterThanOrEqualToThreshold          --dimensions
Name=InstanceId,Value=i-12345678       --evaluation-
periods 1 --alarm-actions arn:aws:automate:us-west-
2:ec2:stop --unit Percent
```

In addition to technical considerations, disaster recovery planning should also address regulatory and compliance requirements, as well as factors such as data privacy and customer trust. Organizations must ensure that their disaster recovery plans comply with relevant industry standards and regulations, such as GDPR, HIPAA, or PCI DSS. AWS CLI commands can be used to configure AWS services in compliance with these standards, such as enabling encryption at rest for Amazon S3 buckets or implementing access controls to restrict data access based on regulatory requirements.

```
bashCopy code
aws s3api put-bucket-encryption --bucket my-bucket --
server-side-encryption-configuration
'{"Rules":[{"ApplyServerSideEncryptionByDefault":{"SSE
Algorithm":"AES256"}}]}'
```

Furthermore, disaster recovery planning should be an ongoing process, regularly reviewed and updated to reflect changes in the organization's IT infrastructure, business priorities, and regulatory landscape. Continuous monitoring and auditing of disaster recovery capabilities are essential to ensure readiness and responsiveness to evolving threats and challenges. AWS CLI commands can automate monitoring tasks by configuring AWS CloudWatch alarms and setting up automated notifications for critical events.

bashCopy code

```
aws cloudwatch put-metric-alarm --alarm-name my-alarm --metric-name CPUUtilization --namespace AWS/EC2 --statistic Average --period 300 --threshold 70 --comparison-operator GreaterThanOrEqualToThreshold --dimensions Name=InstanceId,Value=i-12345678 --evaluation-periods 1 --alarm-actions arn:aws:sns:us-west-2:123456789012:MyTopic --unit Percent
```

In summary, disaster recovery planning and implementation are essential aspects of ensuring business continuity and resilience in the face of unforeseen events. By adopting a proactive approach to disaster recovery and leveraging cloud technologies and automation tools, organizations can effectively mitigate risks and minimize the impact of disasters on their operations. With the flexibility and scalability offered by cloud platforms like AWS, organizations can build robust and resilient disaster recovery solutions tailored to their specific needs and requirements.

Chapter 10: Monitoring and Performance Optimization at Scale

Metrics collection and analysis tools play a pivotal role in monitoring and optimizing the performance, availability, and reliability of systems and applications in modern IT environments. These tools enable organizations to gather, store, analyze, and visualize various types of metrics and telemetry data from different sources, providing valuable insights into the health and behavior of their infrastructure and applications. One widely used open-source tool for metrics collection and monitoring is Prometheus, which is designed to scrape and store time-series data, allowing users to query and visualize metrics using its built-in query language, PromQL. To deploy Prometheus using the command line interface, users can use tools like Docker or Kubernetes. For instance, to deploy Prometheus on Kubernetes, users can create a YAML manifest file defining the Prometheus deployment, service, and persistent volume, and then apply the manifest using the **kubectl apply** command.

bashCopy code

```
kubectl apply -f prometheus.yaml
```

Another popular metrics collection and analysis tool is Grafana, which provides a flexible and intuitive platform for creating dashboards and visualizing metrics from various data sources, including Prometheus, InfluxDB, and Graphite. Grafana's rich set of visualization options and plugins make it a preferred choice for monitoring and troubleshooting complex systems. To install Grafana on a

Linux server, users can use package managers like apt or yum to download and install the Grafana package, and then start the Grafana service using systemd.

bashCopy code

```
sudo apt update sudo apt install grafana sudo systemctl start grafana-server
```

In addition to Prometheus and Grafana, other metrics collection and analysis tools include InfluxDB, Telegraf, and Elasticsearch with Kibana. InfluxDB is a time-series database optimized for storing and querying metrics data, while Telegraf is a lightweight agent that collects system metrics and sends them to InfluxDB. Elasticsearch with Kibana, commonly known as the ELK stack, is a popular choice for log and metrics analysis, offering powerful search and visualization capabilities. To deploy the ELK stack using Docker Compose, users can create a YAML file defining the Elasticsearch, Logstash, and Kibana services, and then use the **docker-compose up** command to start the services.

bashCopy code

```
docker-compose up -d
```

Furthermore, cloud providers offer managed metrics collection and analysis services, such as Amazon CloudWatch, Google Stackdriver, and Azure Monitor. These services enable users to collect, visualize, and analyze metrics and logs from various cloud resources and services, providing a centralized platform for monitoring and troubleshooting cloud-based applications. With AWS CLI, users can create CloudWatch alarms to monitor specific metrics and trigger automated actions based on predefined thresholds.

bashCopy code

```
aws cloudwatch put-metric-alarm --alarm-name my-alarm
--alarm-description "My alarm description" --metric-
name CPUUtilization --namespace AWS/EC2 --statistic
Average --period 300 --threshold 90 --comparison-
operator GreaterThanThreshold --evaluation-periods 2 --
actions-enabled --alarm-actions arn:aws:sns:us-east-
1:123456789012:my-topic
```

In summary, metrics collection and analysis tools are essential components of modern IT infrastructure, enabling organizations to monitor and optimize the performance, availability, and reliability of their systems and applications. Whether deploying open-source solutions like Prometheus and Grafana or leveraging managed services from cloud providers, having robust metrics monitoring capabilities is critical for maintaining the health and efficiency of digital operations.

Continuous performance optimization strategies are essential for maintaining and improving the efficiency, responsiveness, and scalability of software systems over time. These strategies involve a systematic approach to identifying performance bottlenecks, analyzing system behavior, and implementing optimizations to enhance overall performance. One key aspect of continuous performance optimization is monitoring. Effective monitoring provides visibility into the performance metrics of an application or system, allowing teams to identify areas for improvement. Tools such as Prometheus, Grafana, and Datadog are commonly used for monitoring system metrics, resource utilization, and application performance. Using Prometheus, for instance, teams can configure custom metrics and alerts to monitor specific performance indicators, such as response times, error rates, and resource usage. They can deploy Prometheus using Docker or Kubernetes, and then create custom dashboards in Grafana to visualize performance metrics and identify potential bottlenecks.

bashCopy code

```
kubectl apply -f prometheus.yaml
```

Another crucial aspect of continuous performance optimization is profiling and benchmarking. Profiling tools like pprof for Go, YourKit for Java, and py-spy for Python enable developers to analyze the runtime behavior of their applications and identify performance hotspots. By running performance tests and benchmarks using tools like Apache JMeter, wrk, or Siege, teams can assess the impact of code changes on system performance and identify opportunities for optimization. For instance, developers can use Apache JMeter to simulate load on a web application and measure its response time under various traffic conditions.

bashCopy code

```
jmeter -n -t test_plan.jmx -l results.jtl
```

Furthermore, teams can employ techniques such as caching to improve application performance and reduce response times. By caching frequently accessed data or computed results, applications can avoid expensive computations or database queries, thereby improving overall responsiveness. Redis and Memcached are popular caching solutions used to store key-value pairs and session data in memory. To deploy Redis on a server, users can download and install the Redis package using package managers like apt or yum, and then start the Redis server using systemd.

bashCopy code

sudo apt update sudo apt install redis-server sudo systemctl start redis-server

Additionally, employing techniques such as load balancing and horizontal scaling can help distribute incoming traffic across multiple servers and prevent individual servers from becoming overloaded. Load balancers such as NGINX and HAProxy can be configured to distribute incoming requests based on various algorithms, such as round-robin or least connections. To deploy NGINX as a load balancer, users can install the NGINX package and then configure the load balancer settings in the NGINX configuration file.

bashCopy code

sudo apt update sudo apt install nginx

Moreover, continuous performance optimization involves regular code reviews and optimizations to identify and address inefficiencies in the codebase. By analyzing code performance using profiling tools and identifying areas of high CPU usage, memory consumption, or I/O operations, developers can refactor code to improve performance and reduce resource usage. Techniques such as code caching, lazy loading, and asynchronous processing can also be employed to optimize code execution and improve application responsiveness.

Furthermore, leveraging cloud services such as AWS Lambda, Azure Functions, or Google Cloud Functions enables teams to offload compute-intensive tasks to serverless environments, where resources are provisioned dynamically based on demand. This allows applications to scale automatically and efficiently handle fluctuations in workload without manual intervention. To deploy a function on AWS Lambda, users can use the AWS CLI to package and deploy the function code and specify its runtime environment and configuration settings.

bashCopy code

```
aws lambda create-function --function-name my-function --runtime nodejs14.x --handler index.handler --zip-file fileb://function.zip --role arn:aws:iam::123456789012:role/service-role/my-role
```

In summary, continuous performance optimization is a vital aspect of maintaining the efficiency and reliability of software systems. By employing monitoring, profiling, caching, load balancing, code optimization, and serverless computing techniques, teams can identify and address performance bottlenecks, improve application responsiveness, and ensure smooth operation under varying workloads. By integrating performance optimization into the development and deployment pipeline, organizations can deliver high-performance applications that meet the demands of modern users and businesses.

BOOK 4
EXPERT INSIGHTS IN APPLICATION DESIGN
CUTTING-EDGE APPROACHES FOR DATA-INTENSIVE
SYSTEMS

ROB BOTWRIGHT

Chapter 1: Next-Generation Architectural Paradigms

Decentralized and distributed architectures are fundamental concepts in modern computing, playing a crucial role in building resilient, scalable, and fault-tolerant systems. These architectures distribute computational tasks and data across multiple nodes, enabling systems to operate efficiently and reliably in diverse environments. One key characteristic of decentralized architectures is the absence of a single point of control or authority, with decision-making distributed among participating nodes. This decentralization promotes resilience and fault tolerance by reducing the impact of node failures or network partitions. In contrast, distributed architectures involve the coordination and communication of multiple nodes to achieve a common goal, often relying on distributed algorithms and protocols to maintain consistency and synchronization. These architectures are commonly used in various domains, including distributed databases, peer-to-peer networks, blockchain systems, and content delivery networks.

Deploying decentralized and distributed architectures often involves the use of containerization and orchestration technologies such as Docker and Kubernetes. Docker allows developers to package applications and dependencies into lightweight, portable containers, which can then be deployed and run consistently across different environments. To create a Docker container for a decentralized application, developers can write a Dockerfile specifying the application's dependencies and configuration, build the

container image using the Docker build command, and then run the container using the Docker run command.
bashCopy code

```
docker build -t my-decentralized-app . docker run -d my-decentralized-app
```

Kubernetes, on the other hand, provides a platform for automating the deployment, scaling, and management of containerized applications. With Kubernetes, developers can define deployment configurations, specify resource requirements, and define scaling policies using Kubernetes manifests. To deploy a decentralized application on Kubernetes, developers can create Kubernetes manifests for deploying containerized application components, such as pods, services, and deployments, and then apply these manifests using the kubectl apply command.
bashCopy code

```
kubectl apply -f deployment.yaml
```

Decentralized architectures are commonly used in blockchain systems, where multiple nodes collaborate to validate transactions, maintain a distributed ledger, and achieve consensus on the state of the network. In blockchain networks like Bitcoin and Ethereum, each node maintains a copy of the blockchain ledger and participates in the consensus mechanism to validate and add new transactions to the ledger. Consensus algorithms such as Proof of Work (PoW) and Proof of Stake (PoS) are used to ensure agreement among nodes and prevent double-spending and other malicious activities.

Deploying a blockchain network typically involves setting up and configuring blockchain nodes using specialized software such as Geth for Ethereum or bitcoind for Bitcoin. Developers can use CLI commands to initialize a new blockchain node, specify network parameters, and join an existing network as a participant node. For instance, to initialize a new Ethereum node using Geth, developers can run the geth init command to create a new blockchain database and then start the node using the geth --syncmode full command to synchronize with the Ethereum network.

bashCopy code

```
geth init genesis.json geth --syncmode full
```

In addition to blockchain systems, decentralized architectures are also used in peer-to-peer (P2P) networks, where nodes communicate directly with each other to share resources, data, and services. P2P networks like BitTorrent and IPFS enable users to distribute and access content in a decentralized manner, without relying on central servers or intermediaries. In these networks, each node acts as both a client and a server, contributing bandwidth and storage resources to the network while consuming content shared by other nodes.

Deploying a decentralized P2P network involves deploying and configuring P2P software on participating nodes and configuring network settings to enable peer discovery and communication. For instance, in a BitTorrent network, users can create and share torrent files containing metadata about the content to be distributed, and then use BitTorrent client software such as uTorrent or Transmission to download and share files with other peers in the network.

bashCopy code

```
transmission-cli my_file.torrent
```

Overall, decentralized and distributed architectures offer numerous benefits, including resilience, scalability, and fault tolerance, making them well-suited for building resilient and scalable systems in various domains. By leveraging containerization, orchestration, and specialized software tools, developers can deploy and manage decentralized and distributed applications effectively, enabling them to harness the power of decentralized computing for a wide range of use cases.

Hybrid cloud and multi-cloud strategies have emerged as pivotal approaches in modern cloud computing, offering organizations flexibility, scalability, and resilience in managing their IT infrastructure and applications. These strategies involve the integration and utilization of multiple cloud environments, including private clouds, public clouds, and on-premises infrastructure, to optimize performance, cost, and reliability based on specific requirements and workload characteristics. Hybrid cloud architectures enable organizations to leverage the benefits of both public and private clouds, allowing them to run mission-critical workloads on-premises while leveraging the scalability and agility of public cloud services for less sensitive applications or peak workloads.

Deploying a hybrid cloud environment typically involves integrating on-premises infrastructure with public cloud services from providers such as Amazon Web Services (AWS), Microsoft Azure, or Google Cloud Platform (GCP). Organizations can use tools like AWS Outposts, Azure Stack, or Google Anthos to extend their on-premises environment into the respective cloud provider's infrastructure, enabling seamless workload migration, data synchronization, and hybrid cloud management. For example, with AWS Outposts, organizations can deploy

AWS-designed infrastructure on-premises and seamlessly integrate it with their existing AWS cloud environment using the AWS Management Console or AWS CLI.

bashCopy code

```
aws outpost create-outpost --name my-outpost --site-id my-site --availability-zone us-west-2a
```

Multi-cloud strategies, on the other hand, involve the use of multiple cloud service providers to avoid vendor lock-in, enhance resilience, and optimize cost and performance. Organizations may choose to leverage different cloud providers based on factors such as geographic presence, service offerings, pricing models, and regulatory compliance requirements. By distributing workloads across multiple cloud platforms, organizations can mitigate the risk of service outages or performance degradation caused by issues with a single provider and take advantage of specialized services or features offered by different providers.

Deploying a multi-cloud environment requires careful planning and management to ensure interoperability, security, and cost optimization across different cloud platforms. Organizations can use cloud management platforms (CMPs) or multi-cloud management tools to orchestrate workloads, manage resources, and enforce policies across multiple cloud environments. Tools like VMware CloudHealth, CloudCheckr, or Terraform Cloud offer centralized management and visibility into multi-cloud deployments, allowing organizations to monitor performance, track costs, and enforce compliance across disparate cloud environments.

bashCopy code

```
terraform apply -var-file=my_cloud_providers.tfvars
```

One common use case for hybrid and multi-cloud strategies is disaster recovery and business continuity planning. By leveraging both on-premises infrastructure and cloud resources, organizations can implement resilient architectures that ensure data availability and service continuity in the event of a disaster or service outage. For example, organizations can replicate critical data and workloads from on-premises infrastructure to a public cloud environment using data replication tools like AWS Storage Gateway, Azure Site Recovery, or Google Cloud Storage Transfer Service, allowing for rapid failover and recovery in the event of a disaster.

bashCopy code

```
gcloud compute scp my_file.txt gs://my-bucket
```

Moreover, hybrid and multi-cloud architectures enable organizations to optimize cost and performance by dynamically scaling resources based on workload demand and leveraging pricing differences between cloud providers. For example, organizations can use cloud-native autoscaling features or third-party tools like Kubernetes Horizontal Pod Autoscaler (HPA) or AWS Auto Scaling to automatically adjust resource capacity in response to changing workload requirements, ensuring optimal performance and cost efficiency across hybrid and multi-cloud environments.

bashCopy code

```
kubectl autoscale deployment my-deployment --cpu-percent=70 --min=2 --max=10
```

In summary, hybrid cloud and multi-cloud strategies offer organizations the flexibility, scalability, and resilience needed to meet the evolving demands of modern IT environments. By combining on-premises infrastructure with public cloud services and leveraging multiple cloud providers, organizations can optimize performance, enhance resilience, and reduce dependency on any single cloud vendor. With the right tools and management practices, organizations can successfully deploy and manage hybrid and multi-cloud environments to achieve their business objectives and drive innovation in the cloud-native era.

Chapter 2: Advanced Data Processing Techniques

Data streaming and complex event processing (CEP) have become essential components of modern data architectures, enabling organizations to process and analyze vast amounts of data in real-time to extract valuable insights and drive timely decision-making. Data streaming involves the continuous ingestion, processing, and analysis of data records as they are generated, allowing organizations to gain immediate insights and respond to events as they occur. Complex event processing extends this capability by enabling organizations to detect patterns, correlations, and anomalies within streaming data in real-time, enabling them to identify meaningful events and trigger automated actions or alerts based on predefined rules or conditions.

Deploying a data streaming and complex event processing system typically involves the use of specialized platforms and technologies designed to handle the unique requirements of real-time data processing and analysis. Apache Kafka, Apache Flink, and Apache Spark are popular open-source frameworks for building scalable and fault-tolerant data streaming and processing pipelines. These frameworks provide the necessary infrastructure and abstractions for ingesting, processing, and analyzing streaming data at scale, enabling organizations to build real-time applications for various use cases such as fraud detection, predictive maintenance, and personalized recommendations.

bashCopy code

```
kafka-topics --create --topic my-topic --partitions 3 --
replication-factor 2 --bootstrap-server localhost:9092
```

Apache Kafka, in particular, has emerged as a leading distributed streaming platform, providing features such as high-throughput, fault-tolerance, and horizontal scalability for handling large volumes of streaming data. Organizations can deploy Kafka clusters on-premises or in the cloud and use Kafka Connect to integrate with various data sources and sinks, enabling seamless data ingestion and egress from Kafka topics. Kafka Streams and ksqlDB further extend Kafka's capabilities by enabling stream processing and real-time analytics directly within the Kafka ecosystem, allowing organizations to build end-to-end streaming applications without needing to integrate with external processing frameworks.

bashCopy code

```
kubectl apply -f kafka-cluster.yaml
```

In addition to open-source frameworks, cloud-based streaming platforms such as Amazon Kinesis, Google Cloud Pub/Sub, and Azure Event Hubs offer managed services for ingesting, processing, and analyzing streaming data in the cloud. These platforms provide scalability, reliability, and ease of use, allowing organizations to focus on building real-time applications without worrying about managing infrastructure or scalability challenges. Organizations can use CLI commands or web interfaces to provision and configure streaming resources, define data streams, and configure processing pipelines to handle streaming data in the cloud.

bashCopy code

```
aws kinesis create-stream --stream-name my-stream --
shard-count 2 --region us-east-1
```

Complex event processing (CEP) engines play a crucial role in analyzing streaming data and detecting meaningful patterns or events in real-time. Platforms such as Apache Flink, Esper, and Drools provide capabilities for defining event patterns, aggregating data, and triggering actions based on complex event patterns or conditions. These engines can process high-throughput streams of data and perform sophisticated event processing operations such as event correlation, pattern recognition, and temporal reasoning, enabling organizations to identify and respond to critical events or anomalies in real-time.

bashCopy code

```
flink run -m localhost:8081 my-stream-processing-job.jar
```

One common use case for data streaming and complex event processing is real-time monitoring and anomaly detection in IT systems and infrastructure. Organizations can ingest logs, metrics, and events from various sources such as servers, network devices, and applications into a streaming platform and use CEP engines to analyze the data in real-time. By defining rules and thresholds for detecting abnormal behavior or performance issues, organizations can trigger alerts or automated actions to remediate problems before they impact service availability or performance.

bashCopy code

```
kubectl logs my-stream-processing-pod
```

Moreover, data streaming and complex event processing are increasingly being used in IoT (Internet of Things) applications to process sensor data, monitor equipment health, and detect anomalies in industrial and manufacturing environments. By ingesting sensor data streams into a streaming platform and applying CEP rules to detect patterns or anomalies in real-time, organizations can optimize production processes, prevent equipment failures, and improve operational efficiency in IoT deployments.

In summary, data streaming and complex event processing play a critical role in enabling real-time data processing and analysis for a wide range of use cases across industries. By leveraging streaming platforms and CEP engines, organizations can ingest, process, and analyze vast amounts of streaming data in real-time, enabling them to gain immediate insights, detect meaningful events, and trigger automated actions or alerts based on predefined rules or conditions. With the right tools and techniques, organizations can build scalable and resilient streaming pipelines to power their real-time applications and drive innovation in the era of big data and IoT.

Graph processing and analysis have emerged as fundamental techniques for understanding and extracting insights from complex interconnected data structures, such as social networks, biological networks, transportation networks, and recommendation systems. Graphs consist of vertices (nodes) connected by edges (links), representing relationships or interactions between entities. Graph processing involves performing computations and analytics on these graphs to uncover patterns, identify communities, detect anomalies, and derive valuable insights. Deploying graph processing techniques typically involves the use of specialized graph databases, frameworks, and algorithms designed to efficiently store, query, and analyze large-scale graph data.

Graph databases such as Neo4j, Amazon Neptune, and TigerGraph provide dedicated storage and query capabilities optimized for handling graph data. These databases allow organizations to model complex relationships and perform graph traversals, pattern matching, and graph algorithms efficiently. Deploying a graph database involves setting up and configuring the database server, defining the schema and data model, and loading the graph data into the database.

bashCopy code

```
docker run --name neo4j-container -p 7474:7474 -p 7687:7687 -d neo4j
```

Neo4j, for example, is a popular open-source graph database that uses the Cypher query language for performing graph traversals and querying graph data. Organizations can deploy Neo4j clusters on-premises or in the cloud and use Cypher queries to perform various graph analytics tasks such as finding shortest paths, calculating centrality measures, and identifying connected components in the graph.

bashCopy code

```
aws neptune create-db-cluster --db-cluster-identifier my-neptune-cluster --engine-version 1.0.4
```

Amazon Neptune is a fully managed graph database service offered by AWS, providing high availability, durability, and scalability for storing and querying graph data in the cloud. Organizations can use Neptune's API or CLI commands to create and manage graph database clusters, define graph schemas, and execute Gremlin or SPARQL queries to analyze graph data.

Graph processing frameworks such as Apache Giraph, Apache Flink, and Apache Spark GraphX provide distributed computing capabilities for performing large-scale graph analytics on clusters of machines. These frameworks enable organizations to parallelize graph algorithms and analytics tasks across multiple nodes, allowing them to analyze massive graphs efficiently. Deploying a graph processing framework typically involves setting up a distributed computing cluster, deploying the framework's software, and writing graph algorithms using the framework's APIs or libraries.

bashCopy code

```
flink run -m localhost:8081 my-graph-processing-job.jar
```

Apache Flink, for example, is a distributed stream processing framework that supports graph processing through its Gelly library. Organizations can deploy Flink clusters on-premises or in the cloud and use Gelly's APIs to implement and execute graph algorithms such as PageRank, community detection, and graph traversal on large-scale graphs.

Graph algorithms play a crucial role in analyzing and extracting insights from graph data. These algorithms include centrality measures such as degree centrality, betweenness centrality, and closeness centrality, which quantify the importance or influence of nodes in a graph. Community detection algorithms such as Louvain Modularity and Label Propagation help identify densely connected groups or clusters of nodes within the graph, revealing underlying structures or communities.

Anomaly detection algorithms such as Local Outlier Factor (LOF) and Isolation Forest can identify unusual or anomalous patterns in the graph, such as outliers or unexpected connections, which may indicate potential fraud, security breaches, or emerging trends. Pathfinding algorithms such as Dijkstra's algorithm and A* search algorithm enable organizations to find shortest paths between nodes in the graph, facilitating route planning, network optimization, and navigation applications.

Graph analytics applications span various domains, including social network analysis, recommendation systems, fraud detection, cybersecurity, bioinformatics, and knowledge graph construction. In social network analysis, graph algorithms can help identify influential users, detect communities or cliques, and analyze information diffusion or viral spreading dynamics within the network.

In recommendation systems, graph-based approaches such as collaborative filtering and personalized PageRank can be used to generate personalized recommendations by leveraging the relationships between users, items, and their interactions. Graph-based fraud detection systems can analyze the network structure and transaction patterns to detect suspicious activities or fraudulent behavior within financial or social networks.

In cybersecurity, graph analytics techniques can help identify network intrusions, detect malware propagation, and uncover patterns of malicious activities by analyzing the connections and interactions between devices, users, and applications in the network. Bioinformatics applications of graph analytics include analyzing biological networks such as protein-protein interaction networks, gene regulatory networks, and metabolic networks to understand the underlying mechanisms of diseases, drug interactions, and biological processes.

Knowledge graph construction involves integrating and connecting heterogeneous data sources to build a unified graph representation of knowledge, enabling semantic search, question answering, and knowledge discovery applications. By leveraging graph databases, frameworks, and algorithms, organizations can unlock the value of graph data and harness its power to gain deeper insights, make informed decisions, and drive innovation across various domains.

Chapter 3: Machine Learning Integration in Application Design

Machine learning model deployment strategies play a pivotal role in the successful implementation of machine learning solutions in real-world scenarios. Once a machine learning model is trained and evaluated, deploying it into production environments becomes crucial to leverage its predictive capabilities and derive value from the insights it provides. There are various strategies and techniques for deploying machine learning models, each tailored to specific use cases, infrastructure requirements, and operational considerations.

One of the common approaches to deploying machine learning models is through containerization using platforms like Docker and Kubernetes. Docker provides a lightweight, portable containerization solution that encapsulates the model, its dependencies, and runtime environment into a single package, ensuring consistency across different environments.

bashCopy code

```
docker build -t my_model . docker run -p 8080:8080 my_model
```

Using Docker, organizations can package their machine learning models as container images and deploy them to any environment that supports Docker, whether it's on-premises or in the cloud. Kubernetes, on the other hand, enables automated deployment, scaling, and management of containerized applications, including machine learning models, across a cluster of machines.

```bash
bashCopy code
kubectl apply -f deployment.yaml
```
By defining Kubernetes deployment manifests, organizations can specify the desired state of their machine learning model deployments, including the number of replicas, resource constraints, and service configurations, and Kubernetes ensures that the deployed models are resilient, scalable, and highly available.

Serverless computing platforms like AWS Lambda, Azure Functions, and Google Cloud Functions offer another deployment option for machine learning models, allowing organizations to execute code in response to events without provisioning or managing servers.

```bash
bashCopy code
aws lambda create-function --function-name my-function --runtime python3.8 --handler my_function.handler --role arn:aws:iam::123456789012:role/lambda-role --zip-file fileb://function.zip
```
By packaging machine learning models as serverless functions, organizations can achieve auto-scaling, pay-per-use pricing, and seamless integration with other cloud services, making it ideal for event-driven and low-latency inference scenarios.

Model deployment through dedicated model serving frameworks such as TensorFlow Serving, TorchServe, and MLflow provides another option for deploying machine learning models at scale. These frameworks offer specialized model serving capabilities, including model versioning, inference caching, and monitoring, ensuring high-performance, low-latency model inference.

```bash
bashCopy code
```

```
mlflow models serve -m model_uri -h 0.0.0.0 -p 5000
```

MLflow, for example, is an open-source platform for managing the end-to-end machine learning lifecycle, including model deployment and serving. By using MLflow's model serving capabilities, organizations can deploy machine learning models as REST API endpoints, enabling easy integration with existing applications and services.

Model deployment in edge computing environments is another emerging trend, where machine learning models are deployed closer to the data source or end-users to reduce latency, conserve bandwidth, and ensure privacy and security.

```
bashCopy code
docker build -t my_edge_model . docker push
my_edge_model:latest
```

By packaging machine learning models into lightweight containers and deploying them to edge devices such as IoT devices, gateways, and edge servers, organizations can perform real-time inference and decision-making at the edge, enabling edge intelligence and enabling applications such as predictive maintenance, anomaly detection, and autonomous vehicles.

Continuous integration and continuous deployment (CI/CD) pipelines play a crucial role in automating the deployment of machine learning models, ensuring that changes to the model code, data, or configuration are automatically tested, validated, and deployed to production environments.

```
bashCopy code
git push origin main
```

By integrating model training, evaluation, and deployment into CI/CD pipelines using tools like Jenkins, GitLab CI/CD, or GitHub Actions, organizations can achieve rapid iteration, experimentation, and deployment of machine learning models, accelerating time-to-market and improving overall agility.

Model monitoring and observability are essential aspects of model deployment, enabling organizations to track the performance, behavior, and health of deployed models in real-time. By instrumenting models with monitoring hooks and integrating with monitoring and logging platforms such as Prometheus, Grafana, or ELK Stack, organizations can gain insights into model performance, identify drift, and detect anomalies, ensuring the reliability and effectiveness of deployed models.

In summary, deploying machine learning models involves a variety of strategies and techniques, each tailored to specific use cases, requirements, and constraints. By leveraging containerization, serverless computing, model serving frameworks, edge computing, CI/CD pipelines, and model monitoring, organizations can effectively deploy, manage, and scale machine learning models in production environments, unlocking the value of AI and machine learning across various domains and applications.

Federated learning and privacy-preserving techniques represent cutting-edge advancements in the field of machine learning, particularly in scenarios where data privacy and security are paramount concerns. Federated learning allows multiple parties to collaboratively train a shared machine learning model while keeping their data decentralized and private. This approach is particularly

beneficial in situations where data cannot be centralized due to regulatory, privacy, or security constraints. One prominent example of federated learning is Google's Federated Learning framework, which enables mobile devices to collaboratively train a global model while keeping user data on-device. To deploy federated learning, organizations can use frameworks such as TensorFlow Federated (TFF), an open-source framework for federated learning, which provides APIs for defining federated computations, simulations, and experiments.
bashCopy code

```
pip install tensorflow-federated
```

By leveraging TFF, organizations can implement federated learning algorithms, including federated averaging and federated optimization, and deploy federated learning systems across distributed environments such as edge devices, IoT devices, and mobile devices. Another privacy-preserving technique closely related to federated learning is homomorphic encryption, which allows computations to be performed on encrypted data without decrypting it. Homomorphic encryption enables data owners to share encrypted data with third parties, such as machine learning model providers, without compromising data privacy. To deploy homomorphic encryption, organizations can use libraries such as Microsoft SEAL (Simple Encrypted Arithmetic Library), an open-source homomorphic encryption library that enables privacy-preserving computations on encrypted data.
bashCopy code

```
git clone https://github.com/microsoft/SEAL.git cd SEAL/native/src make
```

By integrating Microsoft SEAL into their machine learning pipelines, organizations can perform operations such as addition, multiplication, and convolution on encrypted data, enabling privacy-preserving machine learning tasks such as predictive modeling, classification, and regression. Differential privacy is another privacy-preserving technique that focuses on adding noise to datasets to prevent the leakage of sensitive information about individual data points. Differential privacy mechanisms ensure that the output of machine learning algorithms does not reveal sensitive information about individual data points in the training data. To deploy differential privacy, organizations can use libraries such as TensorFlow Privacy, an extension of TensorFlow that provides tools and techniques for training machine learning models with differential privacy guarantees.

bashCopy code

pip install tensorflow-privacy

By incorporating TensorFlow Privacy into their machine learning workflows, organizations can train models with built-in differential privacy mechanisms, such as Gaussian noise injection and gradient clipping, to ensure that the resulting models are privacy-preserving and robust against privacy attacks. Secure multi-party computation (MPC) is another privacy-preserving technique that enables multiple parties to jointly compute a function over their inputs while keeping their inputs private. MPC protocols ensure that no party learns anything about the inputs of other parties beyond what can be inferred from the output of the computation. To deploy secure multi-party computation, organizations can use libraries such as

PySyft, an open-source framework for privacy-preserving machine learning built on top of PyTorch.

bashCopy code

pip install syft

By leveraging PySyft, organizations can implement MPC protocols, including secure addition, multiplication, and comparison, and deploy privacy-preserving machine learning systems across distributed environments, such as edge devices, cloud servers, and decentralized networks. In summary, federated learning and privacy-preserving techniques represent innovative approaches to addressing privacy and security concerns in machine learning. By deploying federated learning, homomorphic encryption, differential privacy, and secure multi-party computation, organizations can ensure that their machine learning systems are privacy-preserving, secure, and compliant with regulatory requirements, enabling them to unlock the value of sensitive data while respecting user privacy and confidentiality.

Chapter 4: Event-Driven Architectures for Real-Time Analytics

Event sourcing and event-driven microservices are architectural patterns that revolutionize how applications capture, process, and store data by focusing on events as the primary source of truth. Event sourcing is a pattern where the state of an application is determined by a sequence of immutable events, rather than by directly modifying mutable state. This approach enables applications to maintain a complete audit trail of all changes to their state, providing a reliable mechanism for data recovery, auditing, and debugging. To implement event sourcing, developers often use frameworks such as Axon Framework in Java or EventFlow in .NET. These frameworks provide abstractions for defining events, aggregates, and event handlers, making it easier to build event-sourced applications.

bashCopy code

Install Axon Framework mvn install

In an event-driven microservices architecture, services communicate with each other asynchronously through events. Each microservice produces and consumes events, allowing for loose coupling between services and enabling them to scale independently. To deploy event-driven microservices, organizations can use messaging systems such as Apache Kafka, RabbitMQ, or Amazon SQS to facilitate event communication between services. These messaging systems provide durable message storage, message routing, and message delivery guarantees, ensuring that events are reliably processed even in the face of failures.

bashCopy code

```
# Install Apache Kafka brew install kafka
```

Event sourcing and event-driven microservices are closely related and often used together to build scalable, resilient, and maintainable applications. In this architecture, each microservice maintains its own event store, which serves as the source of truth for its state. When an event is produced by a microservice, it is stored in the event store and then published to the message broker for consumption by other services. This ensures that changes to the application state are captured as a series of immutable events, providing a reliable mechanism for data synchronization and consistency across services.

To illustrate the benefits of event sourcing and event-driven microservices, consider an e-commerce application where orders are placed, processed, and fulfilled by multiple microservices. When a new order is placed, an "order created" event is generated by the order service and stored in its event store. This event is then published to the message broker and consumed by other services, such as the inventory service and the payment service. Each service reacts to the event by updating its own state and producing additional events as necessary. For example, the inventory service might decrement the quantity of items in stock, while the payment service might authorize the payment transaction. By using events as the primary means of communication between services, the application becomes more resilient to failures, as events can be replayed to recover lost state and ensure data consistency.

In addition to resilience and consistency, event sourcing and event-driven microservices offer other benefits such as scalability, flexibility, and auditability. Since events are stored in an append-only fashion, the event store can scale horizontally to accommodate high write throughput and large volumes of data. Furthermore, the decoupled nature of event-driven communication allows services to evolve independently, making it easier to introduce new features, refactor existing code, and adapt to changing business requirements. Finally, the auditability of event sourcing enables organizations to trace the full history of changes to their data, providing valuable insights for compliance, debugging, and analytics purposes.

Despite their benefits, event sourcing and event-driven microservices also pose challenges, particularly around data consistency, event ordering, and distributed transactions. Ensuring that events are processed in the correct order and that changes to the application state are atomic and consistent across services requires careful design and coordination. Furthermore, managing the complexity of event-driven architectures, including event schema evolution, versioning, and backward compatibility, can be challenging, especially as the number of services and events grows over time.

In summary, event sourcing and event-driven microservices offer powerful architectural patterns for building scalable, resilient, and maintainable applications. By leveraging events as the primary means of communication and adopting event-driven principles, organizations can design systems that are more loosely coupled, easier to evolve, and better aligned with the principles of domain-driven design. However, implementing event-driven architectures requires careful consideration of trade-offs and challenges, including data consistency, event ordering, and distributed transactions. By addressing these challenges and embracing the principles of event-driven design, organizations can unlock new opportunities for innovation and agility in their software development practices.

Complex Event Processing (CEP) systems are specialized software platforms designed to analyze and process streams of data in real-time to identify meaningful patterns, correlations, and relationships among events. These systems are widely used in various industries such as finance, telecommunications, healthcare, and IoT to detect and respond to complex events or situations as they occur. CEP systems enable organizations to gain insights into their data in real-time, make informed decisions, and take immediate action to capitalize on opportunities or mitigate risks.

CEP systems operate on the principles of event-driven architecture, where events are continuously generated, processed, and analyzed to extract meaningful information. One of the key features of CEP systems is their ability to handle high volumes of data from diverse sources and process it in real-time. To deploy a CEP system, organizations typically install the CEP software on their servers or cloud infrastructure and configure it to ingest data streams from various sources such as sensors, databases, message brokers, or external APIs.

bashCopy code

```
# Install Apache Flink wget https://www.apache.org/dyn/closer.lua/flink/flink-1.14.0/flink-1.14.0-bin-scala_2.12.tgz tar -xzvf flink-1.14.0-bin-scala_2.12.tgz
```

One of the primary use cases for CEP systems is in financial trading, where milliseconds can make the difference between profit and loss. In this context, CEP systems analyze market data feeds, order books, and trade executions in real-time to identify trading opportunities, detect anomalies, and execute trades automatically. For example, a CEP system might detect a sudden increase in trading volume for a particular stock and trigger an automated buy or sell order based on predefined trading strategies.

Another common use case for CEP systems is in telecommunications, where they are used to monitor network traffic, detect network anomalies, and optimize network performance. By analyzing streaming data from network devices, CEP systems can identify patterns indicative of network congestion, cyber-attacks, or hardware failures and take proactive measures to mitigate these issues. For example, a CEP system might detect a sudden spike in data traffic on a cell tower and dynamically reroute traffic to neighboring towers to prevent network congestion.

In healthcare, CEP systems are used to monitor patient vital signs, detect abnormal health conditions, and trigger alerts for medical staff. By analyzing streaming data from medical devices such as heart rate monitors, blood pressure monitors, and oxygen sensors, CEP systems can detect patterns indicative of medical emergencies, such as heart attacks or seizures, and alert medical staff to intervene promptly. For example, a CEP system might detect a sudden drop in a patient's oxygen saturation levels and alert nurses to administer oxygen therapy immediately.

To effectively process streaming data and identify meaningful events, CEP systems employ a variety of techniques such as pattern recognition, rule-based processing, and machine learning algorithms. These techniques enable CEP systems to detect complex patterns and relationships in data streams, such as temporal correlations, spatial relationships, and causal dependencies. By combining multiple techniques, CEP systems can provide rich insights into the underlying data and enable organizations to make informed decisions in real-time.

One of the key challenges in deploying CEP systems is managing the complexity of processing streaming data at scale. As the volume and velocity of data increase, organizations must ensure that their CEP systems can handle the load efficiently and reliably. This often requires deploying CEP systems in distributed architectures and leveraging technologies such as

Apache Flink, Apache Kafka, or Apache Storm to achieve high throughput and low latency processing.

In summary, Complex Event Processing (CEP) systems play a critical role in enabling organizations to analyze and process streaming data in real-time to identify meaningful patterns and events. By leveraging event-driven architecture and advanced analytical techniques, CEP systems empower organizations to gain insights into their data, make informed decisions, and take immediate action to capitalize on opportunities or mitigate risks. However, deploying and managing CEP systems at scale requires careful consideration of factors such as data volume, velocity, and complexity, as well as the selection of appropriate technologies and architectures to meet the organization's requirements.

Chapter 5: Quantum Computing Applications in Data-Intensive Systems

Quantum computing represents a revolutionary approach to computation, leveraging the principles of quantum mechanics to perform complex calculations that are beyond the capabilities of classical computers. At its core, quantum computing harnesses the unique properties of quantum bits, or qubits, to represent and manipulate information in ways that defy classical intuition. Unlike classical bits, which can exist in one of two states (0 or 1), qubits can exist in superpositions of these states, enabling them to represent multiple values simultaneously. This fundamental property forms the basis of quantum parallelism, allowing quantum computers to explore multiple solutions to a problem simultaneously.

To deploy a basic quantum computing environment for experimentation and learning, one can use quantum computing simulators or cloud-based quantum computing platforms. IBM Quantum Experience is a popular platform that provides access to quantum computers via the cloud, allowing users to run quantum circuits and experiment with quantum algorithms.

bashCopy code

```
# Install IBM Quantum Experience CLI pip install qiskit
```

Quantum computing algorithms leverage quantum phenomena such as superposition and entanglement to perform calculations with exponential speedup compared to classical algorithms. One of the most well-known quantum algorithms is Shor's algorithm, which efficiently factors large integers, a problem that is believed to be intractable for classical computers. This algorithm has significant implications for cryptography, as many cryptographic protocols rely on the difficulty of factoring large numbers for their security.

Another prominent quantum algorithm is Grover's algorithm, which provides a quadratic speedup for unstructured search problems. Grover's algorithm can be used to search an unsorted database in $O(\sqrt{N})$ time, compared to the $O(N)$ time required by classical algorithms. This algorithm has applications in optimization, database search, and cryptography.

Quantum computing is still in its early stages of development, and building practical quantum computers capable of outperforming classical computers for a wide range of tasks remains a significant challenge. One of the main obstacles is quantum decoherence, which refers to the loss of quantum coherence due to interactions with the environment. Decoherence introduces errors into quantum computations and limits the size and complexity of quantum algorithms that can be executed reliably.

To address the challenge of quantum decoherence, researchers are exploring various approaches to quantum error correction and fault tolerance. Quantum error correction codes, such as the surface code, can detect and correct errors in quantum computations, thereby mitigating the effects of decoherence. Fault-tolerant quantum computation aims to design algorithms and architectures that can tolerate a certain level of errors and still produce reliable results.

Another area of active research in quantum computing is the development of quantum software and programming languages. Quantum software development frameworks, such as Qiskit, Quipper, and Cirq, provide tools and libraries for designing, simulating, and executing quantum algorithms. These frameworks abstract away the complexities of quantum hardware and allow researchers and developers to focus on algorithm design and optimization.

Despite the current challenges and limitations, quantum computing holds immense promise for revolutionizing various fields, including cryptography, materials science, optimization, and machine learning. Quantum computers have the potential to solve complex problems that are infeasible for classical computers, leading to breakthroughs in areas such as drug discovery, financial modeling, and climate simulation.

In summary, quantum computing represents a paradigm shift in computation, harnessing the principles of quantum mechanics to perform calculations that are beyond the reach of classical computers. While still in its infancy, quantum computing holds the potential to revolutionize numerous fields and solve some of the most challenging problems facing humanity. As research and development in quantum computing continue to advance, we can expect to see increasingly powerful and practical quantum computers that unlock new possibilities for innovation and discovery.

Quantum computing has emerged as a promising avenue for solving optimization and machine learning problems more efficiently than classical computers. Quantum algorithms leverage the principles of quantum mechanics to explore large solution spaces and search for optimal solutions with exponential speedup compared to classical algorithms. One of the most notable quantum algorithms for optimization is the Quantum Approximate Optimization Algorithm (QAOA), which is designed to tackle combinatorial optimization problems.

To deploy a basic quantum computing environment for experimenting with quantum algorithms, one can use simulators like Qiskit or cloud-based platforms like IBM Quantum Experience.

bashCopy code

Install Qiskit for quantum computing simulation pip install qiskit

QAOA is a hybrid quantum-classical algorithm that combines elements of quantum computing with classical optimization techniques. It aims to find approximate solutions to combinatorial optimization problems by preparing a quantum state that encodes the problem's objective function and then measuring certain quantum properties to estimate the optimal solution. The algorithm iteratively adjusts the parameters of the quantum state preparation circuit to improve the quality of the solution.

Another quantum algorithm with applications in optimization is the Quantum Annealing Algorithm, which is implemented on quantum annealers such as those provided by D-Wave Systems. Quantum annealing leverages quantum fluctuations to search for the global minimum of a cost function, making it particularly well-suited for optimization problems characterized by rugged energy landscapes.

In the field of machine learning, quantum algorithms offer the potential to accelerate training and inference tasks for certain types of models. One such algorithm is the

Quantum Support Vector Machine (QSVM), which employs quantum computing techniques to perform classification tasks. QSVM utilizes quantum kernel methods to map classical data points into a high-dimensional quantum feature space, where quantum algorithms can efficiently separate different classes.

Quantum Generative Adversarial Networks (QGANs) represent another class of quantum machine learning algorithms that leverage the principles of quantum mechanics to generate realistic samples from a given probability distribution. QGANs can potentially outperform classical generative models by harnessing quantum parallelism and entanglement to explore high-dimensional data spaces more efficiently.

While quantum algorithms for optimization and machine learning hold great promise, their practical implementation faces several challenges. One major challenge is the requirement for fault-tolerant quantum hardware capable of running complex quantum algorithms reliably. Current quantum computers suffer from errors caused by decoherence and noise, which limit the size and complexity of problems that can be solved.

Furthermore, quantum algorithms often require significant expertise in both quantum mechanics and the specific problem domain to design and implement effectively. As a result, widespread adoption of quantum algorithms for optimization and machine learning may require interdisciplinary collaboration between quantum physicists, computer scientists, mathematicians, and domain experts.

Despite these challenges, research in quantum algorithms for optimization and machine learning is progressing rapidly, fueled by advances in quantum hardware, quantum software development frameworks, and theoretical understanding. As quantum computing technology continues to mature, we can expect quantum algorithms to play an increasingly important role in solving real-world optimization and machine learning problems more efficiently than classical approaches.

Chapter 6: Blockchain Integration for Data Security and Integrity

Smart contracts and decentralized applications (DApps) represent a significant advancement in blockchain technology, enabling the creation of programmable, trustless, and autonomous systems. Smart contracts are self-executing contracts with the terms of the agreement directly written into code, stored and executed on a blockchain. These contracts automatically enforce the rules and conditions of an agreement, eliminating the need for intermediaries and enhancing transparency and security.

To deploy a smart contract on a blockchain network like Ethereum, developers typically use tools like Truffle or Remix, along with the Solidity programming language.

bashCopy code

Install Truffle for smart contract development npm install -g truffle

Smart contracts can be deployed for various purposes, ranging from financial transactions and tokenization to supply chain management and decentralized governance. For example, in the context of financial transactions, smart contracts can be used to facilitate peer-to-peer lending, crowdfunding, or automated investment management without the need for traditional financial intermediaries.

Tokenization refers to the process of representing real-world assets, such as real estate, stocks, or commodities, as digital tokens on a blockchain. Smart contracts can enforce the rules governing the transfer and ownership of these tokens, enabling fractional ownership, increased liquidity, and automated compliance.

Supply chain management is another area where smart contracts can add value by improving transparency, traceability, and efficiency. By recording key supply chain events and transactions on a blockchain, smart contracts can automate processes such as inventory management, product authentication, and quality control, reducing fraud and counterfeit goods.

Decentralized governance refers to systems where decision-making processes are governed by smart contracts and decentralized autonomous organizations (DAOs) rather than centralized authorities. Participants in a decentralized governance system can vote on proposals, allocate resources, and govern the direction of a project or organization without relying on intermediaries or trusted third parties.

Decentralized applications (DApps) are software applications that run on a decentralized network of computers, typically leveraging smart contracts to manage backend logic and data storage. DApps can offer various benefits, including censorship resistance, data privacy, and increased user control over their data.

To interact with DApps, users typically use web browsers with built-in Ethereum wallet extensions like MetaMask, which allow users to securely manage their digital assets and interact with smart contracts directly from their browser.

bashCopy code

```
# Install MetaMask browser extension for interacting with
DApps https://metamask.io/download.html
```

Some examples of DApps include decentralized finance (DeFi) platforms for lending, borrowing, and trading digital assets; decentralized exchanges (DEXs) for trading cryptocurrencies without intermediaries; and decentralized social media platforms for content creation and monetization.

Despite their potential, smart contracts and DApps face several challenges, including scalability, security vulnerabilities, and regulatory uncertainty. Scalability concerns arise from the limited throughput and high transaction fees of existing blockchain networks, which can hinder the widespread adoption of DApps.

Security vulnerabilities, such as smart contract bugs and exploits, pose significant risks to the integrity and functionality of DApps. Developers must follow best practices for smart contract development, such as code audits, formal verification, and testing frameworks, to mitigate these risks.

Regulatory uncertainty surrounding blockchain technology and cryptocurrencies can also impact the adoption and development of smart contracts and DApps. Regulatory frameworks vary widely between jurisdictions, and developers must navigate complex legal and compliance requirements when deploying DApps for real-world use cases.

Despite these challenges, smart contracts and decentralized applications continue to evolve and innovate, driven by the growing demand for trustless, transparent, and censorship-resistant systems. As blockchain technology matures and scalability solutions are implemented, smart contracts and DApps are poised to play an increasingly important role in reshaping various industries and disrupting traditional business models.

Blockchain consensus mechanisms and cryptography are fundamental components that underpin the security, integrity, and decentralization of blockchain networks. Consensus mechanisms are protocols used to achieve agreement among network participants on the validity of transactions and the state of the ledger. Cryptography, on the other hand, provides the cryptographic primitives and algorithms necessary to secure transactions, protect data privacy, and ensure the immutability of the blockchain.

One of the most well-known consensus mechanisms is Proof of Work (PoW), which was popularized by Bitcoin. In PoW, miners compete to solve complex mathematical puzzles in order to add new blocks to the blockchain and validate transactions. The first miner to solve the puzzle and find a valid hash is rewarded with newly minted coins and transaction fees. PoW ensures network security by making it computationally expensive to attack the blockchain, as an attacker would need to control a majority of the network's computational power.

To deploy a Proof of Work blockchain, developers can use frameworks like Bitcoin Core for Bitcoin-based networks or Ethereum for Ethereum-based networks.

bashCopy code

Install Bitcoin Core for deploying a Proof of Work blockchain https://bitcoin.org/en/bitcoin-core/

Another popular consensus mechanism is Proof of Stake (PoS), which is used by blockchain networks like Ethereum 2.0 and Cardano. In PoS, validators are chosen to create new blocks and validate transactions based on the amount of cryptocurrency they hold and are willing to "stake" as collateral. Validators are rewarded with transaction fees and newly minted coins proportional to their stake. PoS is more energy-efficient than PoW since it does not require miners to solve computationally intensive puzzles, but rather relies on economic incentives to secure the network.

To deploy a Proof of Stake blockchain, developers can use tools like Prysm for Ethereum 2.0 or Cardano Node for Cardano.

bashCopy code

```
# Install Prysm for deploying a Proof of Stake blockchain (Ethereum 2.0)
https://docs.prylabs.network/docs/install/install-with-docker/
```

In addition to PoW and PoS, there are other consensus mechanisms such as Delegated Proof of Stake (DPoS), Practical Byzantine Fault Tolerance (PBFT), and Directed Acyclic Graphs (DAGs) like Tangle. Each consensus mechanism has its own advantages and trade-offs in terms of security, scalability, and decentralization, and the choice of consensus mechanism depends on the specific requirements of the blockchain network.

Cryptography plays a crucial role in securing blockchain networks and ensuring the privacy and integrity of transactions. Cryptographic techniques such as hash functions, digital signatures, and cryptographic hash functions are used to achieve these goals. Hash functions are used to map arbitrary data to fixed-size hash values, which are then used to uniquely identify blocks and transactions on the blockchain.

Digital signatures are used to prove the authenticity and integrity of transactions by allowing participants to sign transactions with their private keys, which can then be verified by others using their public keys. This ensures that only the owner of a private key can initiate transactions on the blockchain, preventing unauthorized access and tampering.

To deploy cryptographic techniques in blockchain applications, developers can use cryptographic libraries and frameworks like OpenSSL or the Web3.js library for Ethereum-based applications.

bashCopy code

```
# Install OpenSSL for cryptographic operations
https://www.openssl.org/
```

In addition to hash functions and digital signatures, cryptographic hash functions like SHA-256 are used to secure the immutability of the blockchain by linking blocks together in a chain. Each block contains the hash of the previous block, creating a cryptographic link that makes it computationally infeasible to alter past transactions without also altering all subsequent blocks.

Overall, blockchain consensus mechanisms and cryptography are essential building blocks of blockchain technology, enabling trustless and decentralized systems that can revolutionize various industries and applications. By understanding and leveraging these mechanisms and techniques, developers can build secure, scalable, and robust blockchain networks and applications that meet the needs of users and stakeholders alike.

Chapter 7: Serverless Computing and Function as a Service (FaaS)

Serverless architecture has emerged as a transformative approach to building and deploying applications in the cloud, offering developers the ability to focus on writing code without managing the underlying infrastructure. This paradigm shift from traditional server-based models to serverless computing has revolutionized the way applications are developed, providing scalability, flexibility, and cost-efficiency. Serverless architecture patterns and use cases encompass a wide range of scenarios, each leveraging the benefits of serverless computing to address specific requirements and challenges.

One of the most common serverless architecture patterns is Function as a Service (FaaS), where developers write small, stateless functions that are triggered by events and executed in response to specific requests or events. AWS Lambda, Azure Functions, and Google Cloud Functions are popular FaaS platforms that allow developers to deploy functions without provisioning or managing servers.

bashCopy code

```
# Deploying a function using AWS Lambda CLI aws lambda create-function --function-name my-function --runtime nodejs14.x --handler index.handler --role arn:aws:iam::123456789012:role/lambda-role --zip-file fileb://my-function.zip
```

Use cases for FaaS include real-time data processing, event-driven workflows, and microservices architecture.

For example, a serverless image processing application can use AWS Lambda to resize images uploaded to an S3 bucket, triggering a Lambda function whenever a new image is added.

Another serverless architecture pattern is Backend as a Service (BaaS), which provides pre-built backend functionality such as authentication, data storage, and push notifications, allowing developers to focus on building front-end applications. Services like AWS Amplify, Firebase, and Azure Mobile Apps offer BaaS capabilities, enabling developers to rapidly prototype and deploy mobile and web applications without managing server infrastructure.

bashCopy code

```
# Deploying a backend API using AWS Amplify CLI amplify
add api amplify push
```

Use cases for BaaS include mobile and web applications that require user authentication, data storage, and real-time updates. For example, a serverless chat application can leverage Firebase Authentication for user authentication, Firestore for storing chat messages, and Firebase Cloud Messaging for real-time notifications.

Event-driven architecture is another serverless pattern that leverages event-driven triggers to orchestrate workflows and automate business processes. Services like AWS EventBridge, Azure Event Grid, and Google Cloud Pub/Sub enable developers to decouple components of their applications and react to events in real-time.

bashCopy code

```
# Creating an event rule with AWS EventBridge CLI aws
events put-rule --name my-rule --event-pattern
"{\"source\":[\"aws.s3\"],\"detail-type\":[\"AWS API Call
```

via

CloudTrail\"],\"detail\":{\"eventSource\":[\"s3.amazonaw
s.com\"],\"eventName\":[\"PutObject\"]}}"

Use cases for event-driven architecture include data synchronization, application integration, and workflow automation. For example, a serverless data pipeline can use AWS EventBridge to trigger Lambda functions in response to new data arriving in an S3 bucket, processing and transforming the data before storing it in a database.

Additionally, serverless architecture patterns can be combined with other cloud services to build more complex and scalable applications. For example, a serverless web application can use AWS Lambda for compute, Amazon API Gateway for HTTP endpoints, Amazon DynamoDB for data storage, and Amazon S3 for static content hosting, creating a fully serverless and highly scalable architecture.

In summary, serverless architecture patterns and use cases offer developers a powerful set of tools and services for building scalable, cost-effective, and resilient applications in the cloud. By leveraging FaaS, BaaS, event-driven architecture, and other serverless patterns, developers can focus on delivering value to their users while abstracting away the complexities of managing infrastructure.

Managing state in serverless environments presents unique challenges and opportunities for developers looking to build scalable and resilient applications. Unlike traditional server-based architectures where state can be stored and managed on persistent servers, serverless environments are inherently stateless, meaning they do not maintain any persistent state between invocations. This requires developers to adopt different strategies and techniques for managing state in a serverless context.

One common approach to managing state in serverless environments is to leverage external storage services such as databases, object storage, or key-value stores. These services provide durable storage for application data and can be accessed from serverless functions as needed. For example, Amazon DynamoDB, Azure Cosmos DB, and Google Cloud Firestore are fully managed NoSQL databases that can be used to store and retrieve stateful data in serverless applications.

bashCopy code

```
# Creating a DynamoDB table using AWS CLI aws dynamodb create-table --table-name my-table --attribute-definitions AttributeName=userId,AttributeType=S --key-schema AttributeName=userId,KeyType=HASH --billing-mode PAY_PER_REQUEST
```

By offloading state management to external storage services, developers can ensure data persistence and durability across function invocations, even in the event of function scaling or failures. Additionally, these services offer features such as automatic scaling, replication, and backups, reducing the operational overhead associated with managing stateful data.

Another approach to managing state in serverless environments is to use in-memory caching solutions to temporarily store and retrieve data within function execution contexts. Services like Amazon ElastiCache, Azure Cache for Redis, and Google Cloud Memorystore provide fully managed, scalable, and low-latency caching solutions that can be integrated with serverless applications.

bashCopy code

```
# Creating a Redis cluster using Azure CLI az redis create --name my-redis --resource-group my-resource-group --location eastus --sku Basic --vm-size C0
```

By caching frequently accessed data in memory, developers can improve application performance and reduce latency, especially for read-heavy workloads. However, it's important to consider the transient nature of in-memory caches and ensure that critical data is also persisted to durable storage for long-term reliability.

Serverless applications can also benefit from using state machine orchestrators such as AWS Step Functions, Azure Durable Functions, and Google Cloud Workflows to manage complex workflows and state transitions. These services allow developers to define stateful workflows as state machines, with each state representing a specific step or task in the workflow.

bashCopy code

```
# Creating a Step Functions state machine using AWS CLI aws stepfunctions create-state-machine --name my-state-machine --definition file://state-machine-definition.json --role-arn arn:aws:iam::123456789012:role/step-functions-role
```

State machine orchestrators provide built-in support for managing state transitions, retries, error handling, and parallel execution, making it easier to build and orchestrate complex business processes in serverless applications. By abstracting away the complexity of state management, developers can focus on defining the logic of their workflows and let the orchestrator handle the state transitions.

Additionally, serverless applications can use event-driven architectures to manage state through event sourcing and event-driven triggers. By emitting events from various sources such as API Gateway, S3, or message queues, serverless functions can react to changes in state and update external systems accordingly.

bashCopy code

```
# Publishing an event using Amazon EventBridge CLI aws
events put-events --entries file://event.json
```

Event-driven architectures enable loose coupling between components of a system, allowing for greater flexibility, scalability, and resilience. By decoupling stateful operations from the core logic of serverless functions, developers can design more modular and maintainable applications.

In summary, managing state in serverless environments requires a combination of different strategies and techniques tailored to the specific requirements of each application. By leveraging external storage services, in-memory caching, state machine orchestrators, and event-driven architectures, developers can build scalable, resilient, and efficient serverless applications that effectively manage state across function invocations.

Chapter 8: Edge Computing Strategies for Low-Latency Processing

Edge computing infrastructure and deployment models have emerged as critical components in modern distributed systems, offering unique advantages and challenges for organizations seeking to optimize their computing resources and deliver low-latency applications and services to end-users. At its core, edge computing extends the traditional centralized cloud model by bringing compute, storage, and networking resources closer to the point of data generation and consumption, enabling faster data processing, reduced latency, and improved reliability. One of the key aspects of edge computing is its diverse deployment models, each tailored to specific use cases and requirements.

One prominent edge computing deployment model is the fog computing paradigm, which extends the edge beyond traditional data centers to include intermediary devices such as routers, switches, and gateways. This distributed approach enables data processing and analysis to occur closer to the data source, reducing the need to transmit large volumes of data back to centralized cloud servers. Fog computing leverages existing network infrastructure and edge devices to deliver compute and storage capabilities at the network edge, enabling real-time data processing for applications such as industrial IoT, smart cities, and autonomous vehicles.

bashCopy code

Deploying a fog computing solution with Cisco Kinetic Edge and Fog Processing Module docker run -d --name kinetic-edge-fpm ciscokinetic/edge-fpm:latest

Another edge computing deployment model is the use of edge data centers, which are purpose-built facilities located in close proximity to end-users or IoT devices. These data centers host compute, storage, and networking resources and are interconnected with the broader cloud infrastructure to provide seamless integration and workload migration. Edge data centers are ideal for latency-sensitive applications that require high availability and real-time responsiveness, such as content delivery networks (CDNs), video streaming, and online gaming.

bashCopy code

Provisioning an edge data center with Equinix Metal equinix-metal device create --project my-project --facility ny2 --plan c3.large.x86 --os flatcar --billing hourly

In addition to fog computing and edge data centers, another edge deployment model gaining traction is edge computing at the device level, where compute and storage capabilities are embedded directly into IoT devices, sensors, and endpoints. This approach eliminates the need for centralized processing and enables edge devices to perform real-time analytics and decision-making at the edge of the network. Edge computing at the device level is well-suited for use cases such as predictive maintenance, remote monitoring, and asset tracking, where real-time insights are critical for operational efficiency and business continuity.

bashCopy code

Deploying edge computing software on IoT devices with AWS IoT Greengrass aws greengrass create-device-definition --name my-device-definition --initial-version '{"devices": [{"thingArn": "arn:aws:iot:us-east-1:123456789012:thing/my-device"}]}'

Moreover, a hybrid edge-cloud deployment model combines the benefits of edge computing with the scalability and flexibility of the cloud. In this model, compute tasks are dynamically distributed between edge devices and centralized cloud infrastructure based on workload characteristics, resource availability, and network conditions. This dynamic allocation of compute resources allows organizations to optimize performance, cost, and scalability while ensuring seamless operation across distributed environments.

bashCopy code

Implementing a hybrid edge-cloud deployment with Google Cloud IoT Edge gcloud iot devices create my-device --project=my-project --region=us-central1 --registry=my-registry --device-type=gateway

Furthermore, edge computing infrastructure can be deployed using container orchestration platforms such as Kubernetes, which provide tools for managing and scaling containerized workloads across distributed edge nodes. By containerizing edge applications and deploying them as microservices, organizations can achieve greater flexibility, portability, and resource utilization, while also simplifying deployment and management tasks.

bashCopy code

Deploying edge applications with Kubernetes on edge nodes kubectl apply -f edge-application.yaml

In summary, edge computing infrastructure and deployment models offer a diverse range of options for organizations looking to optimize their distributed computing environments and deliver low-latency applications and services to end-users. Whether leveraging fog computing, edge data centers, device-level edge computing, hybrid edge-cloud deployments, or container orchestration platforms, organizations can benefit from improved performance, reduced latency, and increased agility in meeting the demands of modern digital experiences.

Edge AI and machine learning at the edge have emerged as transformative technologies that enable intelligent decision-making and real-time data processing directly on edge devices, bringing computational capabilities closer to the data source and reducing reliance on centralized cloud infrastructure. By deploying AI and machine learning models at the edge, organizations can achieve low-latency inferencing, reduce bandwidth usage, enhance privacy and security, and enable offline operation in resource-constrained environments.

Edge AI and machine learning models are typically deployed using lightweight frameworks and optimized algorithms tailored to the constraints of edge devices, such as limited processing power, memory, and energy resources. These models are trained using traditional machine learning techniques or more advanced deep learning methods, depending on the complexity of the problem and the availability of labeled data. Once trained, the models are converted into optimized formats such as

TensorFlow Lite, ONNX, or TensorFlow.js for deployment on edge devices.

bashCopy code

Training a machine learning model with TensorFlow on Google Colab !pip install tensorflow

pythonCopy code

```
import tensorflow as tf from tensorflow import keras #
Define and compile a simple neural network model model
=       keras.Sequential([       keras.layers.Dense(128,
activation='relu',                  input_shape=(784,)),
keras.layers.Dense(10,       activation='softmax')       ])
model.compile(optimizer='adam',
loss='sparse_categorical_crossentropy',
metrics=['accuracy']) # Train the model on the MNIST
dataset       model.fit(x_train,       y_train,       epochs=5,
batch_size=32)
```

Once the model is trained and optimized, it can be deployed to edge devices using various deployment techniques and tools. For example, TensorFlow Lite provides a lightweight runtime for running TensorFlow models on edge devices such as smartphones, IoT devices, and microcontrollers. Similarly, ONNX Runtime enables the deployment of models in the Open Neural Network Exchange (ONNX) format to a wide range of edge devices and platforms.

bashCopy code

```
# Convert a TensorFlow model to TensorFlow Lite
tensorflow-lite-convert     --input_model=model.h5     --
output_model=model.tflite
```

bashCopy code

```python
# Convert a PyTorch model to ONNX format
torch.onnx.export(model, input_data, 'model.onnx')
```

In addition to model deployment, edge AI and machine learning at the edge require efficient data preprocessing and feature extraction to optimize model performance and resource utilization. Edge devices often have limited storage and processing capabilities, necessitating the use of lightweight preprocessing techniques such as data compression, feature scaling, and dimensionality reduction. These preprocessing steps can be performed directly on edge devices using specialized libraries and frameworks, such as TensorFlow Data Validation and TensorFlow Transform.

pythonCopy code

```python
# Perform data preprocessing with TensorFlow Transform
import tensorflow_transform as tft def
preprocessing_fn(inputs): outputs = inputs.copy()
outputs['feature1'] =
tft.scale_to_z_score(outputs['feature1'])
outputs['feature2'] = tft.bucketize(outputs['feature2'],
num_buckets=10) return outputs # Apply preprocessing
to input data transformed_dataset = (raw_data,
raw_data_metadata)                                    |
tft.TransformDataset(preprocessing_fn)
```

Moreover, edge AI and machine learning applications often require continuous monitoring and management to ensure optimal performance and reliability over time. Edge devices may experience fluctuations in network connectivity, hardware failures, or changes in operating conditions, necessitating proactive monitoring and automated remediation strategies. Tools such as

TensorFlow Serving and TensorFlow Lite Monitoring enable real-time model monitoring, versioning, and health checks to ensure that deployed models meet performance and accuracy requirements.

bashCopy code

```
# Deploy a TensorFlow Lite model with TensorFlow Lite
Serving tensorflow-lite-serve --model=model.tflite --port=8501
```

bashCopy code

```
# Monitor TensorFlow Lite model performance with
TensorFlow Lite Monitoring tensorflow-lite-monitor --model=model.tflite --logdir=logs
```

In summary, edge AI and machine learning at the edge represent a paradigm shift in how AI and machine learning capabilities are deployed and utilized in distributed computing environments. By leveraging lightweight models, efficient preprocessing techniques, and continuous monitoring and management tools, organizations can harness the power of AI and machine learning directly on edge devices, enabling intelligent decision-making, real-time insights, and enhanced user experiences in a wide range of edge computing applications.

Chapter 9: AI-Driven Automation in Application Deployment and Management

AI-powered DevOps and Continuous Integration/Continuous Deployment (CI/CD) are revolutionizing software development practices by leveraging artificial intelligence (AI) techniques to automate and optimize various aspects of the DevOps lifecycle. These technologies enable organizations to accelerate the delivery of high-quality software products while improving efficiency, reliability, and scalability. AI-powered DevOps encompasses a wide range of use cases, including code analysis, testing, deployment automation, monitoring, and incident response, all of which contribute to the seamless integration and continuous delivery of software updates.

One of the key areas where AI is making a significant impact in DevOps is in code analysis and quality assurance. By using machine learning algorithms, developers can analyze code repositories, identify potential bugs, security vulnerabilities, and code smells, and provide actionable insights to improve code quality. Tools like SonarQube, DeepCode, and CodeClimate leverage AI-powered static code analysis techniques to automatically detect issues and suggest fixes, helping developers write cleaner, more maintainable code.

bashCopy code

Analyze code quality with SonarQube sonar-scanner -Dsonar.projectKey=my_project_key -Dsonar.sources=.

bashCopy code

Use DeepCode CLI for static code analysis deepcode analyze

```bash
Copy code
```

Check code quality metrics with CodeClimate codeclimate analyze --dev

In addition to code analysis, AI is also being used to automate and optimize the testing process in CI/CD pipelines. AI-powered testing frameworks, such as Applitools and Testim, utilize machine learning algorithms to perform intelligent test case generation, test prioritization, and test result analysis, allowing organizations to achieve faster test execution and more accurate test coverage. These tools can automatically identify areas of the application that are most susceptible to defects and prioritize test cases accordingly, enabling efficient use of testing resources and reducing time-to-market.

```bash
Copy code
```

Perform visual testing with Applitools Eyes CLI applitools run

```bash
Copy code
```

Execute AI-powered tests with Testim CLI testim run

Furthermore, AI-powered DevOps enables organizations to automate and streamline the deployment process through intelligent deployment strategies and release management techniques. By leveraging AI algorithms, deployment tools such as Jenkins, GitLab CI/CD, and CircleCI can analyze historical deployment data, identify patterns, and make predictive recommendations for optimizing deployment schedules, resource allocation, and rollback strategies. This helps organizations achieve faster and more reliable deployments while minimizing downtime and mitigating risks.

bashCopy code

Automate deployments with Jenkins pipeline pipeline { agent any stages { stage('Build') { steps { // Build your application } } stage('Test') { steps { // Run tests } } stage('Deploy') { steps { // Deploy to production } } } }

bashCopy code

Configure CI/CD pipeline with GitLab CI/CD .gitlab-ci.yml

bashCopy code

Define workflows with CircleCI configuration .circleci/config.yml

Moreover, AI-powered DevOps enables organizations to implement intelligent monitoring and incident response mechanisms to proactively detect and address issues in production environments. By leveraging AI algorithms for anomaly detection, log analysis, and predictive analytics, monitoring tools such as Prometheus, Grafana, and New Relic can automatically identify abnormal behavior, alert operators, and recommend remedial actions to prevent service disruptions and optimize system performance.

bashCopy code

Monitor system metrics with Prometheus and Grafana docker-compose up -d

bashCopy code

Analyze logs with New Relic Logs newrelic logs

bashCopy code

Set up alerts and notifications in Grafana

Overall, AI-powered DevOps and CI/CD represent a paradigm shift in software development and delivery, enabling organizations to achieve greater agility, efficiency, and reliability in their software development processes. By harnessing the power of AI and machine learning, organizations can automate tedious tasks, optimize workflows, and make data-driven decisions to deliver high-quality software products faster and more efficiently than ever before.

Autonomous systems and self-healing infrastructure represent the pinnacle of modern IT operations, where intelligent automation and advanced algorithms enable systems to operate with minimal human intervention and maintain high availability and reliability. These technologies leverage artificial intelligence (AI), machine learning (ML), and advanced analytics to continuously monitor, analyze, and optimize infrastructure components, allowing organizations to achieve greater efficiency, resilience, and scalability in their operations.

The foundation of autonomous systems lies in their ability to automate routine tasks and adapt to changing conditions without human intervention. This automation is facilitated by various tools and platforms that enable organizations to define and orchestrate workflows, configure infrastructure resources, and deploy applications using code-driven approaches. Infrastructure as Code (IaC) tools like Terraform, Ansible, and AWS CloudFormation allow operators to define infrastructure configurations in declarative or imperative formats and provision resources using standardized templates.

bashCopy code

Provision infrastructure with Terraform terraform apply

bashCopy code

Automate infrastructure configuration with Ansible
ansible-playbook playbook.yml
bashCopy code
Define AWS resources with CloudFormation templates
aws cloudformation create-stack --template-body
file://template.yml

Furthermore, autonomous systems leverage advanced monitoring and telemetry capabilities to collect and analyze vast amounts of data from various sources, including system metrics, logs, and events. Monitoring tools such as Prometheus, Grafana, and Datadog enable organizations to gain real-time visibility into the performance and health of their infrastructure, detect anomalies and performance bottlenecks, and trigger automated responses based on predefined thresholds or conditions.

bashCopy code
Set up monitoring with Prometheus and Grafana
docker-compose up -d
bashCopy code
Monitor infrastructure with Datadog datadog-agent run

Moreover, autonomous systems employ machine learning algorithms to predict and prevent potential issues before they occur, thereby minimizing downtime and ensuring continuous operation. These algorithms analyze historical data, identify patterns and trends, and make predictions about future events, enabling operators to take proactive measures to mitigate risks and optimize system performance. Tools like Amazon SageMaker, Google Cloud AI Platform, and Azure Machine Learning provide platforms and services for training and deploying ML models to automate decision-making processes in autonomous systems.

bashCopy code

```
# Train machine learning models with Amazon SageMaker
aws sagemaker create-training-job --algorithm arn:aws:sagemaker:us-east-1:865070037744:algorithm/scikit-learn-bg-nf
```

bashCopy code

```
# Deploy ML models with Google Cloud AI Platform
gcloud ai-platform models create my_model --regions us-central1
```

bashCopy code

```
# Use Azure Machine Learning to automate ML workflows
az ml pipeline create --name my_pipeline --file pipeline.yml
```

Furthermore, self-healing infrastructure is a key component of autonomous systems, enabling systems to detect and respond to failures automatically. Self-healing mechanisms leverage techniques such as redundancy, failover, and auto-scaling to maintain service availability and performance in the face of failures or disruptions. High-availability configurations, load balancers, and auto-scaling groups are common features of self-healing infrastructure architectures, allowing systems to dynamically adjust resource allocation and distribution based on demand and capacity.

bashCopy code

```
# Configure high-availability architecture with AWS Auto Scaling
aws autoscaling create-auto-scaling-group --auto-scaling-group-name my-group --min-size 2 --max-size 10
```

bashCopy code

```
# Set up load balancing with AWS Elastic Load Balancer
aws elb create-load-balancer --load-balancer-name my-
load-balancer                                    --listeners
"Protocol=HTTP,LoadBalancerPort=80,InstanceProtocol=H
TTP,InstancePort=80" --subnets subnet-12345678
```
bashCopy code
```
# Enable auto-scaling with Google Cloud Managed
Instance Groups gcloud compute instance-groups
managed create my-group --size=2 --template=my-
template --zone=us-central1-a
```

In summary, autonomous systems and self-healing infrastructure represent the future of IT operations, enabling organizations to achieve greater efficiency, resilience, and scalability in their operations. By leveraging automation, AI, and ML, organizations can automate routine tasks, optimize resource allocation, and respond to failures automatically, thereby improving service availability, reducing downtime, and enhancing the overall reliability of their infrastructure.

Chapter 10: Ethics and Governance in Emerging Technologies

Responsible AI and ethical AI development practices are crucial aspects of building AI systems that prioritize fairness, transparency, accountability, and privacy. These principles guide the development, deployment, and use of AI technologies to ensure that they benefit society while minimizing potential harms and risks. Organizations and developers must adopt responsible AI practices to build trust with users, stakeholders, and regulators and to address societal concerns about the ethical implications of AI.

One fundamental aspect of responsible AI development is ensuring fairness and avoiding bias in AI algorithms and models. Fairness concerns arise when AI systems produce discriminatory outcomes, favoring certain groups or individuals over others based on factors such as race, gender, or socioeconomic status. To address this, developers must carefully consider the training data used to train AI models, identify potential biases, and implement techniques such as bias mitigation algorithms and fairness-aware evaluation metrics to mitigate bias and ensure equitable outcomes.

```bash
bashCopy code
# Analyze dataset for bias using IBM AI Fairness 360 toolkit pip install aif360
```

```bash
bashCopy code
# Mitigate bias in AI models with TensorFlow Fairness Indicators pip install fairness-indicators
```

Transparency and explainability are also essential principles of responsible AI development. Users and stakeholders must understand how AI systems make decisions and why certain outcomes are produced. Techniques such as model interpretability, model documentation, and algorithmic transparency enable developers to explain the rationale behind AI decisions and provide users with insights into how models work. Tools like SHAP (SHapley Additive exPlanations) and LIME (Local Interpretable Model-Agnostic Explanations) allow developers to generate explanations for individual predictions and highlight the features that influence model outputs.

bashCopy code

```
# Generate explanations for AI models with SHAP pip
install shap
```

bashCopy code

```
# Explain individual predictions with LIME pip install lime
```

Another critical aspect of responsible AI development is ensuring accountability and mitigating potential risks associated with AI systems. Developers must establish mechanisms for monitoring, auditing, and validating AI systems' behavior throughout their lifecycle to identify and address issues such as model drift, data poisoning, and adversarial attacks. Techniques such as model monitoring, data validation, and robustness testing help detect anomalies and ensure that AI systems operate safely and reliably in real-world environments.

bashCopy code

```
# Monitor AI model performance with TensorFlow Model
Monitoring pip install tensorflow_model_monitoring
```

bashCopy code

```
# Validate input data for AI models using TensorFlow Data
Validation pip install tensorflow_data_validation
```

Moreover, privacy and data protection are critical considerations in responsible AI development. Developers must adhere to data privacy regulations and industry best practices to protect sensitive information and ensure user privacy. Techniques such as data anonymization, differential privacy, and federated learning enable organizations to leverage data while preserving privacy and confidentiality. Privacy-preserving tools and frameworks like PySyft and OpenMined facilitate secure and privacy-preserving AI development by enabling encrypted computation, secure multi-party computation (MPC), and decentralized training.

bashCopy code

```
# Implement federated learning with TensorFlow
Federated pip install tensorflow-federated
```

bashCopy code

```
# Secure multi-party computation with PySyft pip install
syft
```

Furthermore, responsible AI development requires ongoing engagement with stakeholders, including users, policymakers, and civil society organizations, to ensure that AI systems align with societal values and address ethical concerns. Organizations must establish governance structures and mechanisms for ethical review, oversight, and accountability to ensure that AI development processes are transparent, inclusive, and responsive to societal needs and concerns. Engaging in open dialogue and collaborating with diverse stakeholders can help identify and address ethical considerations and build public trust in AI technologies.

In summary, responsible AI and ethical AI development practices are essential for building AI systems that promote fairness, transparency, accountability, and privacy. By adhering to principles such as fairness, transparency, accountability, and privacy, developers can build AI systems that benefit society while minimizing potential harms and risks. Adopting responsible AI practices not only enhances trust in AI technologies but also ensures that AI systems contribute to positive social outcomes and address societal needs and concerns.

Regulatory compliance and legal considerations play a critical role in the development and deployment of emerging technologies, ensuring that innovations adhere to applicable laws, regulations, and standards. As technology continues to advance rapidly, policymakers and regulators are faced with the challenge of updating existing laws and frameworks to address new technologies' unique characteristics and potential risks. For organizations and developers working with emerging technologies, navigating the complex regulatory landscape is essential to mitigate legal risks, protect intellectual property, and build trust with users and stakeholders.

In many jurisdictions, emerging technologies such as artificial intelligence (AI), blockchain, and biotechnology are subject to a patchwork of regulations that may vary significantly across industries and regions. Understanding the regulatory environment relevant to specific technologies and applications is crucial for compliance. For example, in the field of AI, regulations related to data privacy, algorithmic transparency, and discrimination may apply, depending on the nature of the AI system and its intended use cases.

bashCopy code

```
# Check GDPR compliance for AI applications using IBM AI Fairness 360 toolkit  pip install aif360
```

bashCopy code

```
# Ensure compliance with HIPAA regulations for healthcare AI solutions  pip install hipaa-compliance
```

One of the key regulatory considerations in emerging technologies is data protection and privacy. Laws such as the European Union's General Data Protection Regulation (GDPR) and the California Consumer Privacy Act (CCPA) impose strict requirements on the collection, processing, and storage of personal data. Organizations must implement measures to safeguard user privacy, obtain informed consent for data collection and processing, and provide individuals with control over their personal information. Compliance with data protection regulations often involves implementing data encryption, pseudonymization, access controls, and data retention policies.

bashCopy code

```
# Encrypt sensitive data using OpenSSL encryption  openssl enc -aes-256-cbc -in input.txt -out encrypted.txt
```

bashCopy code

```
# Implement pseudonymization with Python pandas library  pip install pandas
```

Another important legal consideration in emerging technologies is intellectual property (IP) protection. Innovations in areas such as AI, biotechnology, and blockchain may involve novel algorithms, inventions, or designs that are eligible for patent protection.

Organizations must carefully manage their IP assets, including filing patents, trademarks, and copyrights, to prevent unauthorized use or infringement by competitors. Additionally, navigating IP licensing agreements, open-source licenses, and technology transfer agreements is essential for collaborating with third parties and commercializing innovations.

```bash
# Search for existing patents using Google Patents search
https://patents.google.com/
```

```bash
# Register trademarks with the United States Patent and Trademark Office (USPTO)
https://www.uspto.gov/trademarks-application-process/filing-online
```

Moreover, emerging technologies often raise novel ethical and societal concerns that policymakers and regulators seek to address through legislation and governance frameworks. For example, AI systems may raise questions about accountability, transparency, and bias, leading to calls for ethical AI guidelines and regulatory oversight. Similarly, developments in areas like biotechnology and gene editing prompt discussions about bioethics, informed consent, and the responsible use of technology.

```bash
# Implement ethical AI principles with TensorFlow Ethical AI Toolkit pip install ethical-ai
```

```bash
# Engage with stakeholders to develop ethical guidelines and governance frameworks
```

Furthermore, international collaboration and standardization efforts are essential for harmonizing regulatory approaches and facilitating cross-border cooperation in emerging technologies. Organizations such as the International Organization for Standardization (ISO) and the International Electrotechnical Commission (IEC) develop standards and guidelines to promote interoperability, safety, and security in emerging technology domains.

```bash
Copy code
# Access ISO standards for emerging technologies
https://www.iso.org/standards.html
```

```bash
Copy code
# Participate in standardization working groups and committees
```

In summary, regulatory compliance and legal considerations are paramount in navigating the complex landscape of emerging technologies. By understanding and adhering to applicable laws, regulations, and standards, organizations can mitigate legal risks, protect intellectual property, and foster trust with users and stakeholders. Moreover, engagement with policymakers, regulators, and standardization bodies is essential for shaping regulatory frameworks that promote innovation while safeguarding societal values and interests. Ultimately, responsible development and deployment of emerging technologies require a proactive approach to compliance and an ongoing commitment to ethical and legal principles.

Conclusion

In summary, the "Application Design: Key Principles for Data-Intensive App Systems" book bundle offers a comprehensive exploration of foundational principles, advanced techniques, and expert insights essential for designing and scaling data-intensive applications. Throughout the four books included in this bundle, readers have been introduced to the fundamental concepts and methodologies underpinning the design and architecture of data-intensive systems.

In Book 1, "Foundations of Application Design: Introduction to Key Principles for Data-Intensive Systems," readers were provided with a solid grounding in the fundamental principles of application design, including data modeling, architecture patterns, and design considerations for scalability and reliability. This introductory book served as a cornerstone for understanding the key concepts that underpin the subsequent volumes.

Building upon this foundation, Book 2, "Mastering Data-Intensive App Architecture: Advanced Techniques and Best Practices," delved into more advanced topics, including distributed systems, microservices architecture, and optimization strategies for handling large-scale data workloads. Through real-world examples and case studies, readers gained a deeper understanding of how to design robust and scalable architectures that meet the demands of modern data-intensive applications.

Book 3, "Scaling Applications: Strategies and Tactics for Handling Data-Intensive Workloads," focused specifically on the challenges of scaling applications to handle increasing data volumes and user traffic. Readers learned about effective scaling strategies, performance optimization techniques, and how to leverage cloud computing and containerization technologies to achieve scalability and resilience.

Finally, Book 4, "Expert Insights in Application Design: Cutting-Edge Approaches for Data-Intensive Systems," provided readers with valuable insights from industry experts and thought leaders in the field of application design. Through interviews, case studies, and analysis of emerging trends, readers gained a deeper understanding of the latest approaches and innovations shaping the future of data-intensive application development.

Collectively, these four books offer a comprehensive and holistic perspective on application design for data-intensive systems, equipping readers with the knowledge, skills, and strategies needed to architect, build, and scale robust and resilient applications in today's data-driven world. Whether you are a seasoned software engineer, an architect, or a technology leader, this book bundle provides valuable insights and practical guidance to help you navigate the complexities of designing and scaling data-intensive applications effectively.